Ann
Upd

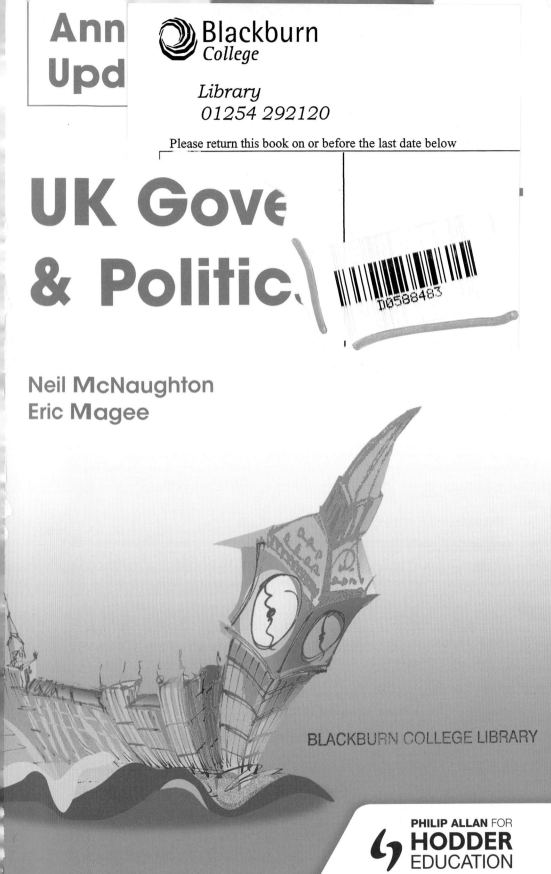

⊚ **Blackburn**
College

Library
01254 292120

Please return this book on or before the last date below

UK Gove
& Politic

Neil **McNaughton**
Eric **Magee**

BLACKBURN COLLEGE LIBRARY

PHILIP ALLAN FOR
↳ **HODDER**
EDUCATION
AN HACHETTE UK COMPANY

Blackburn College	
BB36145	
BBfS	30.01.2014
320.941	£8.99

Philip Allan, an imprint of Hodder Education, an Hachette UK company, Market Place, Deddington, Oxfordshire OX15 0SE

Orders

Bookpoint Ltd, 130 Milton Park, Abingdon, Oxfordshire OX14 4SB
tel: 01235 827827
fax: 01235 400401
e-mail: education@bookpoint.co.uk

Lines are open 9.00 a.m.–5.00 p.m., Monday to Saturday, with a 24-hour message answering service. You can also order through the Philip Allan website: www.philipallan.co.uk

© Neil McNaughton, Eric Magee 2014

ISBN 978-1-4718-0469-4

First printed 2014

Impression number 5 4 3 2 1

Year 2017 2016 2015 2014

All rights reserved; no part of this publication may be reproduced, stored in a retrieval system, or transmitted, in any other form or by any means, electronic, mechanical, photocopying, recording or otherwise without either the prior written permission of Philip Allan or a licence permitting restricted copying in the United Kingdom issued by the Copyright Licensing Agency Ltd, Saffron House, 6–10 Kirby Street, London EC1N 8TS.

Typeset by Integra Software Services Pvt. Ltd., Pondicherry, India

Printed by CPI Group (UK) Ltd, Croydon, CR0 4YY

Hachette UK's policy is to use papers that are natural, renewable and recyclable products and made from wood grown in sustainable forests. The logging and manufacturing processes are expected to conform to the environmental regulations of the country of origin.

P2270

Contents

Chapter 1

2013 elections: who won and does it matter?

Exam success

The up-to-date facts, examples and arguments in this chapter will help you to produce good-quality answers in your AS unit tests in the following areas of the specifications:

Edexcel	AQA	OCR
Unit 1	**Unit 1**	**Unit F851**
Elections	Participation and voting	Participation and voting
	Voting behaviour	Voting behaviour

Context

Elections were held on 2 May 2013 in one Welsh and 35 English local authorities. The results were remarkable for a number of reasons that are discussed in this chapter. Of course, local elections are not the same as national elections so we must be cautious in drawing too many conclusions. The turnout at such elections is very low and people are aware that they are not electing a national government. In addition, there are often local issues that affect local results, as one would expect.

Nevertheless, we can look for some clues in the results and possibly predict some movements in the fortunes of the parties that might take place in years to come, especially in the 2015 general election.

At the same time several localities held mayoral elections. These are also examined below.

The local elections

The results

Table 1.1 shows the results in terms of each party's share of the national vote and also the extent to which this share had changed since the last set of local election results in England and Wales.

Table 1.1 English local government election results, May 2013

Party	% of total vote	Change since 2011 (%)
Labour	29	−8
Conservative	25	−13
UKIP	23	+20
Liberal Democrat	14	−2
Others and independents	9	−3

Table 1.2 shows the number of council seats won by each party and how many each party had won or lost since the last elections.

Table 1.2 Council seats won and lost by the parties, May 2013

Party	Council seats won	Seats won or lost
Conservative	1116	−335
Labour	538	+291
Liberal Democrat	352	−124
Independents	165	+24
UKIP	147	+139
Green	22	+5
BNP	0	−3
Others	21	+4

What happened to the main parties?

Below we examine in turn what these election results have meant for the parties.

UKIP

At first sight it was the UK Independence Party that was the big winner. In terms of the popular vote it came a close third and challenged the two main parties' dominance. The party eclipsed the Liberal Democrats. It gained 139 council seats but failed to gain overall control (i.e. win a majority) of any single council. Although it made these gains its support remains rather too scattered for it to make significant progress. It also has to be remembered that this was a classic 'mid-term election'. Governments are often unpopular between elections, and the electorate uses local elections, as well as other polls such as by-elections, to express their dissatisfaction with the government. Thus the Conservatives and Liberal Democrats were bound to lose votes to UKIP. This suggests it is a 'protest party'. Ironically, the Liberal Democrats used to be the traditional protest party, gaining votes in local elections but losing them again at the general election.

Labour

The party did well enough but its performance was disappointing. Labour was expected to win a much bigger share of the vote and gain many more seats.

The poor opinion poll ratings for its leader, Ed Miliband, were seen as the cause of this modest result. The main opposition party usually makes big gains at mid-term elections. These were disappointing results for Labour.

Conservatives

As expected this was a poor result for the Conservatives. As noted above, governing parties normally lose local government seats in mid term. It was, perhaps, not as bad as they feared. In fact, one could even argue, given the poor state of the economy and falling standards of living, that this was quite a good result for the party.

Liberal Democrats

They were the big losers. Local government is considered a stronghold for Liberal Democrats and they used to control a good number of councils.

What they said

After the election there were reactions from leading members of the main parties. Among the comments were these. After each one there is a suggestion of what these statements really mean if we read between the lines.

Nigel Farage

> It's been a remarkable result for us...we have always done well in European elections but people haven't seen us as relevant to local elections or, in some ways, general elections. So for us to be scoring, on average, 26% of the vote, where we stand is, I think, very significant indeed. This wave of protest certainly isn't short term, it's lasting.

Between the lines: at last we have broken away from being merely an anti-Europe party and are beginning to have a more general appeal. We can convert protest votes into permanent support.

David Cameron

> I understand why some people who have supported us before didn't support us again. They want us to do even more to work for hard-working people....They will be our focus but we have got to do more...of course it is no good insulting a party [UKIP] that people have chosen to vote for...we need to show respect for people who have taken the choice to support this party [UKIP] and we are going to work really hard to win them back.

Between the lines: the Conservatives cannot ignore the result. UKIP has to be taken seriously. In that case Cameron is signalling that perhaps the Conservative Party will have to shift a little to the right to attract UKIP voters.

Nick Clegg

> The Liberal Democrats are on a journey. We're on a journey from a party of protest to a party of government...we're holding our own. The message that only the Liberal Democrats can be relied upon to build a stronger economy and a fairer society, is a message which, where we communicate it successfully, gains support for us.

Between the lines: this is a temporary setback on the road to making the Liberal Democrats electable. He is desperately hoping that the Liberal Democrat 'achievements' will eventually be recognised and the electorate will forget the perceived failures.

Ed Miliband

> I also recognise...the vote for UKIP, the two thirds that didn't vote and that there are still lots of people saying 'can anyone turn this country round?'...It is clear there is more work to do. Our task is to win the trust of the people we haven't yet persuaded that Labour can make a difference.

Between the lines: Miliband was clearly disappointed. The voters are showing dissatisfaction with all those who hold power, but are still not convinced that Labour is the answer to their dissatisfaction.

Summary

It is fairly clear that the only winner of the 2013 local elections was UKIP. Arguably, all the other parties were losers, though one can make a case for arguing that the Conservative Party held its ground as it did not lose as many votes and seats as expected. The second question is **does it matter?** We can divide this answer into two parts. It matters in some senses, but not in others:

It matters because:

- It does indicate how much progress UKIP is making.
- UKIP's success may well affect Conservative policy, shifting it to the right on such issues as Europe, immigration and law and order.
- It demonstrates that Labour is failing to make significant progress. This may cause changes of policy and could undermine Ed Miliband's position as leader.
- It shows that the unpopularity of the Liberal Democrats is persistent and may carry through to 2015 and the general election.

It does not matter because:

- It was not a general election; that election is still over a year away.
- Local elections are used by voters to protest against the government. They may well shift back to their long-term party support in the general election.
- Local government has little autonomy. The shift in control of many local councils from one party to another may not have much effect on communities as it is *national* policies that tend to determine how local government works.

The mayoral elections

There were only two mayoral elections in 2011. The small number was because local referendums indicated that very few localities actually wanted an elected mayor. The two results were as follows:

Doncaster	**Ros Jones (Labour)** elected on the second ballot.
North Tyneside	**Norman Redfearn (Labour)** elected on the second ballot.

So, at first sight these were good results for Labour, but the facts suggest another conclusion. These are safe Labour areas so their candidates were almost bound to win. More importantly, however, the turnout at these elections was very low — 27.2% in Doncaster and 31.8% in North Tyneside. This suggests there is widespread apathy over elected mayors.

Overall conclusion

However much we may analyse the 2013 local and mayoral elections, there is one overwhelming conclusion. **The biggest loser was democracy itself**. The local election turnout was only 31% (down from 42.6% in 2011), which, added to the poor mayoral turnouts, suggests that there is a real participation crisis in Britain in 2013–14.

Exam focus

To consolidate your knowledge of this chapter, answer the following questions:

1 Can local elections tell us anything about the probable result of future general elections?
2 Do the 2013 local elections represent a real breakthrough for UKIP?
3 Are local elections relevant to UK democracy?
4 Has the introduction of elected mayors enhanced democracy in the UK?

Chapter 2

UKIP: a new political force or merely a protest group?

Exam success

The up-to-date facts, examples and arguments in this chapter will help you to produce good-quality answers in your AS unit tests in the following areas of the specifications:

Edexcel	AQA	OCR
Unit 1	**Unit 1**	**Unit F851**
Party policies and ideas	Political parties	Political parties

Context

The UK Independence Party came into existence in 1993, founded by right-wing historian Alan Sked. It was a direct result of the signing of the Maastricht Treaty by Prime Minister John Major in 1992, which transferred a great deal of sovereignty from the UK to the European Community (now called the European Union). It sprang from a pressure group, the Anti-Federalist League, which had been founded in 1991. The current leader, Nigel Farage, was one of the founder members.

Despite its name as a party, it was originally a pressure group as it pursued one overwhelming objective — to bring the United Kingdom out of the European Union. However, by calling itself a party, and by putting up candidates for election, it blurred the lines between what is a party and what is a pressure group. During the 1997 general election, James Goldsmith, a wealthy businessman, formed another party called the Referendum Party, which campaigned, as its name suggested, for a referendum on Britain's membership of the EU. This overshadowed UKIP as Goldsmith was able to purchase a great deal of publicity for his new party. UKIP therefore did not put up any candidates in that year. The Referendum Party offered 547 candidates in 1997 but won only 2.6% of the popular vote and no seats. However, Goldsmith died shortly afterwards and the party collapsed. UKIP then took over as the main anti-European force outside the mainstream parties.

In the early years of the twenty-first century the party made steady progress in terms of membership and votes won at various elections. This was despite the fact that it was threatened by leadership battles and internal strife over tactics and objectives. In particular, the former Labour MP, Robert Kilroy-Silk, a controversial talk-show host, tried to take over the party in 2004. His unstable reputation held the party back and it made only modest progress in the 2005 general election. Nigel Farage provided some stability as leader from 2006 to 2009 and has done so again since 2010 after a brief period under Malcolm Pearson. By 2013 UKIP was beginning to make a serious impact in British politics and Nigel Farage had become a significant political personality.

UKIP's electoral performance

The rise of UKIP can best be seen in terms of its performance in various elections since 1999. A selection of these can be seen in Table 2.1.

Table 2.1 The rise of UKIP, 1999–2013

Year	Type of election	% votes won by UKIP	Seats won by UKIP
1999	European Parliament	7.0	3
2001	General	1.5	0
2004	European Parliament	16.1	12
2005	General	2.3	0
2009	European Parliament	16.5	13
2010	General	3.1	0
2011	Oldham by-election	5.8	0
2011	Barnsley by-election	12.2	0
2012	Rotherham by-election	21.7 (coming second)	0
2013	Eastleigh by-election	27.8 (coming second)	0
2013	Local councils	23.0	147

We can see that the real breakthrough for UKIP came in 2004 when the party won 16.1% of the votes and 12 seats in a European election. Elections to the European Parliament use the highly proportional list system and so small parties have a greater chance of winning seats. By contrast, UKIP has made slower progress in general elections where the electoral system works against it. It cannot realistically win seats under first-past-the-post until its support becomes more concentrated in some constituencies or reaches above 20% of the total vote. Nigel Farage is now talking up the party's prospects of actually coming top of the poll in the 2014 elections to the European Parliament.

UKIP policies

Originally, as we have seen, UKIP was only an anti-European pressure group, which was calling itself a party and putting up candidates at various elections to bring Europe to the top of the political agenda. The main effect of this was to give comfort to the anti-European wing of the Conservative Party by demonstrating how much public support there was for its views. Under Farage's leadership, however, the party has gradually expanded its aspirations.

Farage understood that, if UKIP was to become a genuine force in British politics, it had to break out of its concentration on the issue of Europe and develop policies

across the full range of government responsibilities. Put another way, the party now seeks to dominate the 'right wing' of British politics. Its main policies in 2013 are summarised below.

Europe
UKIP wishes to see Britain withdraw from the European Union altogether. However, it accepts that there needs to be a referendum on the issue. Even if the British people voted to stay in, UKIP would propose a renegotiation of membership and considerable sovereignty returned to the UK.

The economy and taxation
UKIP expects a considerable dividend for Britain if it withdraws from the EU. This should be used to attack the deficit and reduce taxation. The party proposes that the low paid should pay no taxes at all (the tax-free allowance set at minimum wage) and all others should pay a flat rate of income tax. Taxes on business should be reduced, notably employers' contribution to National Insurance and corporation tax. Public expenditure should be curbed by reducing government regulation and waste.

Welfare
The party supports the welfare state but would bear down more severely on benefit cheats and use the money saved to improve care of the elderly and others in need.

Immigration
There should be tight controls on immigration, with only workers with special skills of which there is a shortage in the UK being allowed entry. The rules on asylum seekers should be radically restrictive and migrants from the EU should not have automatic entry to the UK. Immigrants already here should be offered assisted repatriation.

Law and order
There should be significant increases in the size of the police force with more 'bobbies on the beat'. Punishments for serious crimes should be increased and less 'community sentencing' used. There should be a particular campaign against anti-social behaviour.

Environment
The green belt should be protected. The party opposes the use of onshore wind farms and the development of HS2. Local communities should have the power to protect their own environment.

Government
There should be a restoration of local government powers. Further devolution should be opposed.

Foreign policy
On the whole, UKIP is isolationist in its approach and belives that, other than in exceptional circumstances, Britain should not involve itself in military interventions abroad.

Nigel Farage

When Farage first became UKIP leader in 2006 he was not taken very seriously, either by the political community or by the general public. He was seen as something of a stuntman, who went out of his way to shock rather than to present himself as a responsible politician. This image reached a head during the 2010 election campaign when his private plane crashed and he was photographed in the wreckage.

Since then, however, his star has risen along with UKIP's electoral fortunes. Once he had persuaded his party to develop a much wider range of policies, attracted a number of wealthy donors and expanded the membership, he had to be taken more seriously. He still enjoys being pictured with a pint in one hand and a cigarette in the other (partly as a protest against alcohol and tobacco taxes and partly as a protest against what he sees as the persecution of smokers) and he is still prone to making over-provocative remarks, but he is now seen as a genuine threat to the mainstream parties. He has been firm in ridding his party of suspected racists and bigots and in engaging in debate with the other party leaders. In summary, he is what is known as a 'populist' leader, a politician whose appeal tends to chime with many people's basic emotions.

He does have a major problem though, which is that UKIP still looks like a one-man band. The party has no other high-profile leaders and he has not been able to attract many important defectors from the Conservative Party. The question may well be how well he can debate with the other leaders in a general election campaign. As things stand, he remains both UKIP's main asset and also its greatest problem.

Box 2.1	The things he says: some of Nigel Farage's recent statements

I have become increasingly used to the Tory party mimicking our policies and phrases in a desperate effort to pretend to their members they are still Eurosceptic.

The banking collapse was caused, more than anything, by bad government policy and the total failure of bad regulation, rather than by greed.

It's about mass immigration at a time when 21% of young people can't find work. It's about giving £50 million a day to the EU when the public finances are under great strain.

Having established that good ideas do indeed come in from the cold, start on the fringes and become mainstream, can we make any predictions about what the next move will be?

We're no longer just saying who should be running Britain — we're now saying how Britain should be governed.

I think that politics needs a bit of spicing up.

UKIP and the Conservative Party

There is no doubt that UKIP now represents a threat to the fortunes of the Conservative Party. While UKIP may take votes away from the other two main parties, it is the Tories who have most to fear. Commentators point to what happened to Labour in 1981 when a moderate splinter group turned itself into a new party — the Social Democrat Party (SDP). As a result, Labour support among voters was divided and it suffered two huge defeats in 1983 and 1987. A similar fate could befall the Conservatives. The main dangers for the Conservatives from UKIP are as follows:

- By attracting the votes of disaffected Conservatives, it will split the right-wing vote and prevent many Conservative candidates winning seats where there is a 'conservative' majority in the constituency.
- UKIP is exposing divisions within the Conservative Party. The more radical Eurosceptics fear the influence of UKIP and so are pushing the leadership to hold a referendum on membership and to take a harder line on European issues. In general, UKIP may be pushing the Conservatives to more right-wing positions, so threatening some support for the Conservatives in the country.
- UKIP may begin to win members from the Conservative Party, whose membership is already dropping alarmingly.
- It may be that some Conservative MPs or peers will defect to UKIP in the future.

Summary

The European election of 2014 and the general election of 2015 are likely to prove to be the key moments in the life of UKIP. As UKIP always does well in European elections it is likely to do well in the 2014 European election, but it is yet to make a breakthrough in domestic politics. It also needs to win seats in the House of Commons. This is a high hurdle to jump. It will probably need popular support of at least 20% to achieve any representation.

However, we should emphasise the impact the party has had, especially on the Conservatives. UKIP can legitimately claim to have influenced Conservative Party policy in the following areas:

- UK relations with the EU and the possibility of a referendum on continuing British membership
- immigration and the idea of much tighter controls, even over migrants from within the EU, and possibly repatriation of some groups
- the adoption of a harder line on benefit claimants
- a tougher line on law and order issues

If UKIP is a new political force, it will have to start winning seats in Westminster, not just in the European Parliament and in local elections. If it does not, it will remain a protest group. As a protest group it can claim great success in placing various issues high on the political agenda and in influencing the Conservative Party, but it is still not a successful party in the full meaning of the term.

In summary, therefore, to be called a major political force UKIP must:

- Start to win seats at Westminster. In order to do this, it needs to attract former Labour and Liberal Democrat voters as well as disillusioned Conservative supporters.
- Establish Nigel Farage as a credible party leader.
- Develop a coherent political programme.
- Rid itself of its so-called 'lunatic fringe'.

Exam focus

To consolidate your knowledge of this chapter, answer the following questions:

1 What are the distinctions between a party and a pressure group, and why is the distinction sometimes blurred?
2 What do you understand by the term 'right wing' in British politics?
3 Why do small parties have difficulty in gaining representation in the UK?
4 Is Britain now a multi-party system?

Chapter 3

Political parties: are they ideology-free zones?

Exam success

The up-to-date facts, examples and arguments in this chapter will help you to produce good-quality answers in your AS unit tests in the following areas of the specifications:

Edexcel	AQA	OCR
Unit 1	**Unit 1**	**Unit F851**
Party policies and ideas	Political parties	Political parties

Context

Until the 1990s political parties in the UK were heavily influenced by political ideologies and their policies were largely based in such ideas. By 'ideology' here we mean fundamental principles that propose specific reforms to society and include a vision of what an 'ideal' society will look like. The main ideologies that flourished in British politics were **democratic socialism** (a less extreme form of socialism), **liberalism** and **'New Right'** conservatism. Traditional conservatives, by contrast, opposed such ideological politics and sought to find a consensus, which avoided too many inflexible principles.

In practice, this meant that there was also a good deal of fundamental conflict between the parties. Such conflict reached a head in the early 1980s, when the Conservative Party fell under the influence of Margaret Thatcher, who developed her own ideological position based on neo-liberalism and neo-conservatism, while the Labour Party veered to the left and campaigned for socialist ideas in direct conflict with Thatcherism. At the same time, both the Labour Party and the newly formed Social Democrat Party (which became the Liberal Democrats in 1988) adopted liberal positions, especially on legal, social and moral issues. The Thatcherite conservatives often criticised these liberal ideals.

In the 1990s, however, both main parties began to moderate their policies and so became less ideological. John Major (prime minister, 1990–97) started the process among the Conservatives, while Labour was transformed into 'New Labour', a much less ideological movement, under John Smith (leader, 1992–94) and Tony Blair (leader, 1994–97; prime minister, 1997–2007). This process of 'emptying' British party politics of ideological content has carried on since.

This chapter seeks to understand how ideology has declined in the political process and asks to what extent the parties retain some ideological positions. It also asks whether ideological conflict may be starting to return, especially as Ed Miliband adopts increasingly 'left-wing' positions, as the right-wing Conservatives begin to increase their influence (encouraged by the rise of UKIP), and as there is growing tension between liberalism and the forces of conservatism in general.

What ideologies?

Before we seek answers to the questions above, we need to be clear what ideological positions we are referring to. These include the following three traditions.

Democratic socialism

Democratic socialism includes such ideals as:

- Some redistribution of income from rich to poor through taxation and welfare.
- A very strong commitment to a state-run welfare system.
- The pursuit of equal legal, social and economic rights for all sections of society.
- The creation of equality of opportunity for all.
- The maintenance of strong trade unions to protect the interests of workers.
- Where necessary, there should be regulation of capitalism to ensure it operates in the interests of the whole community.
- Where it is in the public interest, some industries should be publicly owned and run by the state on behalf of the community.

Liberalism

Liberalism includes these ideals (several in common with democratic socialism):

- The power of the state should be limited and controlled by the rule of law, a strong constitution, an independent judiciary and a powerful parliament.
- Civil rights and individual liberties should be safeguarded, preferably by a binding set of codified rights.
- There should be equal rights for all individuals and groups in society.
- Different cultures, lifestyles and ethnic or religious groups should be tolerated and allowed to flourish together (multiculturalism).
- There should be social justice, ensuring that wealth and income in the economy are distributed on the basis of merit rather than simply market power.
- Support for the welfare state.

'Thatcherite' conservatism

'Thatcherite' conservatism includes these ideals:

- A belief in free markets (i.e. free from distortions created by government interference or by powerful trade unions) in goods, labour and finance.
- Government interference in markets is usually counter-productive and inhibits enterprise and wealth creation.
- Taxes on personal incomes and on business should be kept as low as possible.
- Welfare benefits should be kept at a minimum to avoid a 'dependency culture'.
- Government should behave responsibly with the public finances and avoid excessive public debt.

- A hard line should be taken on law and order issues, with an emphasis on punishment and deterrence rather than rehabilitation and attacking the causes of crime.
- The services of the welfare state can be provided by either the state or the private sector, depending on which is more efficient and gives better value for money.
- A belief in international trade free from the excessive interference of the European Union.

Traditional conservatism (also known as 'one nation conservatism', or even 'liberal conservatism') is not considered an ideology. Such conservatives oppose ideological politics, are suspicious of radical reform in society and prefer to seek a consensus before developing new policies. Under David Cameron, this wing of conservatism has become dominant, though the right-wing 'Thatcherite' faction (which calls itself the representative of true, fundamental conservatism) is growing in strength and influence.

To what extent are the three main parties 'ideological' today?

Tables 3.1, 3.2 and 3.3 summarise the position of the main parties in turn, outlining which of their current principal policies can be described as 'ideological' in nature, based on fundamental principles and ideals, and which are not but can be described as pragmatic, flexibly based and consensual, i.e. seeking the non-ideological middle ground.

Table 3.1 Labour Party policies

Ideological	Non-ideological
• Under Miliband the party proposes closer regulatory controls on large-scale capitalist enterprises, notably in terms of pricing and taxation.	• Labour does not propose to restore the powers of trade unions, which were lost in the 1980s.
• Miliband has also proposed in 2013 that land that is lying unused and is suitable for building could be nationalised (publicly owned and state-run) and brought into use.	• There is an acceptance that free market capitalism remains the main way to create wealth.
• Through tax credits, minimum wage and other benefits the party is pursuing the idea of a minimum living wage for all.	• Despite being committed to the welfare state, the party now accepts that the private sector can play a role in providing services.
• The party remains committed to education as the vehicle for creating equality of opportunity.	• Labour now accepts that business enterprise is the source of economic growth and prosperity, and so must not be over-taxed in case incentives are destroyed.
• Labour proposes a more graduated income tax system to reduce inequality, notably increasing taxes on the wealthy.	• A policy announced in October 2013 accepts that private groups of parents should be able to establish schools.
• The party remains committed to anti-discrimination policies.	• Labour has accepted increased university tuition fees despite their adverse effect on equality of opportunity.

Table 3.2 Conservative Party policies

Ideological	Non-ideological
• The party is still committed to state deregulation and low taxes in business. • There is a firm belief in the maintenance of free product, labour and financial markets. • Conservatives are highly critical of a welfare benefits system that discourages work and enterprise and encourages dependency. • Direct taxes are seen as a disincentive to work, enterprise and investment and so should be kept at as low a level as possible. • Government should avoid public sector excessive debt and should pursue a 'balanced books' policy. • The party still sees property ownership as a key element in a secure and prosperous society.	• Despite its commitment to private sector enterprise, the party accepts the need for a mixture of private and public sector services, notably in health, education and social care. • The party has resisted the idea of flat-rate direct taxes, which would promote inequality. It accepts that inequality in the UK should be reduced by various means. • The party accepts that there is a consensus in the UK on such issues as equal rights, non-discrimination and tolerance, and so pursues policies to foster them. • Similarly, the party accepts that there is a need to make the UK constitution more democratic and accessible, and so has promoted (mostly unsuccessfully) some constitutional reform.

Table 3.3 Liberal Democrat Party policies

Ideological	Non-ideological
• Liberal Democrats will not tolerate any weakening in measures that protect the rights and liberties of individuals. • The party remains committed to social justice (less inequality and rewards based on merit), although it has made compromises under the coalition. • Equality of opportunity is a key goal (again, despite compromises). • The party supports various constitutional reforms to make the UK more democratic, to decentralise government, to limit the power of government and to protect rights more effectively. • The party strongly supports the maintenance of all aspects of the welfare state.	• The Liberal Democrats have had to make many concessions in order to protect the coalition, so many of its ideological positions have been 'watered down'. • The party has adopted a consensus, middle-ground position on the control of the excesses of capitalism. • The party formerly adopted a liberal attitude to law and order issues, concentrating on crime prevention and rehabilitation. It now takes a centrist approach, differentiating between serious and petty crime. • It accepts that welfare state provisions can be provided by a mixture of the private and public sectors.

We need to add a word of caution here. The apparent 'consensus' between Conservatives and Liberal Democrats may turn out to be false. It exists to maintain the coalition. Therefore, if and when the current coalition comes to an end, we may have a better indication of whether the Liberal Democrats will restore their pure liberal ideals. The same has been much less true of the Conservatives under coalition, though they have had to take a less rigid stance on European issues and have been unable to reform the tax system as they would wish in deference to liberal democrat principles.

Consensus politics and managerialism

The rise of consensus politics since the 1990s has given rise to the idea of 'managerialism'. This implies that the parties compete not so much on the basis of different, contrasting policies, as on their claims to be able to 'manage' Britain more effectively. For example, all three parties agree that reducing or eliminating the government budget deficit is a key goal of government. The left-wing factions in Labour and the Liberal Democrats may disagree that this is a priority, but it is part of mainstream politics in all parties. Therefore, the parties vary little on exactly how they would reduce the deficit, concentrating more on how quickly and how well they would do so. On the whole, Labour tends to favour higher taxation to restore a balanced budget, while Conservatives seek more to reduce public spending in order to do the same. Similar kinds of analysis can be applied to the management of the benefits system, the environment, education, and health and social care.

So, where consensus, non-ideological inter-party politics prevail, managerialism becomes more important. There may *appear* to be great conflict between the parties, but this does not run very deep and does not signify a great deal of ideological conflict. Put simply, **the parties argue about means rather than ends**.

Ideology and adversary politics

By contrast, when parties disagree over *ends* and not just *means* we experience ideological conflict. This is often described as adversary politics. Here the arguments run deep and are fundamental. Arguably, politics in the UK over the past 60 years or so has passed through four phases:

1 **1951–63:** consensus politics — little ideological conflict

2 **1964–92:** adversary politics based on fundamental ideological differences

3 **1992–2012:** a return to largely non-ideological politics

4 **2012–present:** signs of a possible return to ideological politics:
   • conservatism versus liberalism
   • democratic socialism versus Thatcherism

Summary

It remains to be seen, especially from 2015 onwards, whether the signs of ideology creeping into party politics will develop further. For now, in 2014, we can summarise the extent to which there is a broad non-ideological consensus between the main parties and the extent to which some ideological conflicts remain. Table 3.4 includes some, but not all of such conflicts.

Table 3.4 Examples of consensus issues and ideological differences, 2014

Consensus issues	Ideological conflict areas
■ All parties are committed to better emissions control, development of sustainable energy sources and anti-climate change policies. They do have some disagreements over how to achieve these ends. ■ They agree about the need to reduce the public sector deficit and move towards a more balanced government budget. ■ All parties agree that the basic principles and quality of welfare state services, including health, education and social care, should be maintained. ■ The three main parties now agree that there need to be greater controls on immigration and asylum seeking, concentrating on attracting only those immigrants and migrants who can contribute to British society. ■ There is agreement that there should be greater safeguards against those who are abusing the benefits system.	■ There are differences over the extent and ways in which large-scale capitalist enterprises should be controlled, especially banking and utilities. ■ The Conservatives disagree with Labour and the Liberal Democrats over how progressive the income tax system should be, especially how much of the tax burden should fall on the wealthy. ■ There remain fundamental differences over what the UK's relationship with the EU should be. ■ The Conservatives are now arguing that there is an excessive culture of protecting individual rights in the UK, to the detriment of anti-crime and terrorism measures. Labour and the Liberal Democrats disagree.

The term 'ideology-free zone' has looked appropriate to British party politics over recent decades. However, we should be alert to the very real possibility that ideological politics may be returning in the years to come.

Exam focus

To consolidate your knowledge of this chapter, answer the following questions:

1 Distinguish between consensus and adversary politics.
2 To what extent has the Conservative Party abandoned Thatcherite principles?
3 To what extent has the Labour Party abandoned democratic socialist principles?
4 To what extent are the Liberal Democrats still 'liberal'?
5 Explain three consensus issues in UK politics.
6 Explain three UK political issues that are subject to adversary politics.

Chapter 4

Welfare reform: real change or just cost-cutting?

Exam success

The up-to-date facts, examples and arguments in this chapter will help you to produce good-quality answers in your AS unit tests in the following areas of the specifications:

Edexcel	AQA	OCR
Unit 1	**Unit 1**	**Unit F851**
Political parties	Political parties	Political parties

Context

Beginning in 2013 the government is implementing a major reform of the welfare benefits system in the UK. Most of the measures were contained in the **Welfare Reform Act** of 2012. This is one of the most ambitious reforms of the welfare system since the creation of the welfare state in the 1940s.

At the same time, the coalition government is engaged in a desperate attempt to reduce the government deficit — the amount the government has to borrow annually in order to make up the gap between its tax receipts and its expenditure programmes. The deficit ballooned during the economic and financial crisis that began in 2008 and started to threaten the long-term prosperity and financial stability of the UK.

This chapter looks at both aspects of government policy and poses the question of whether the two are linked. In other words, is the plan to reduce spending on welfare benefits a *genuine* reform, or is it little more than part of the grand plan to reduce the deficit? Of course, it is impossible to give a definitive answer because no minister would ever admit to such a link, while opposition politicians are bound to make such claims. We can, though, look at some of the evidence.

What are the welfare reforms?

The main reforms to the benefits system are as follows.

Universal credit

This replaces a number of separate tax credits available for those who are out of work or living on low incomes. It is being gradually introduced starting in 2013. This will save money in two ways. First, it simplifies an existing range of benefits and will be easier to claim. This will reduce administration costs. Second, it will create an incentive for people to find work in low-paid jobs because it will 'top up' their earnings and make work worthwhile (added to the raising of the tax-free threshold to £10,000 per annum by 2015). Clearly, if unemployment falls as a result, expenditure on benefits will also fall.

Total benefit cap

A total benefit cap is being introduced from spring 2013 onwards. This is a highly controversial measure for those on the left of British politics as it may reduce the standard of living of many people on benefits. It does not apply to disability benefits and a few other essential benefits. In 2013 it has been set at £500 per week per family where there are two parents or in lone-parent families. For single individuals without dependent children it stands at £350 per week. It is designed to reduce expenditure and to answer critics who say that some families are living too well on benefits and have no incentive to find work.

Personal Independence Payments (PIP)

These are being introduced from April 2013 onwards. They grant payments to all adults who have special disability problems. The size of the payments will be based on the level of disability and the special needs of individuals. It replaces the former Disability Living Allowance (DLA), which was less focused on specific needs. The new allowances will cost government much less than the DLA.

Employment and Support Allowance (EWA)

This replaces a range of current disability payments. They will be based on a new Work Capability Assessment (WCA). This will require those claiming disability benefit to be assessed to see whether they can work at all and/or what kind of work they could do, given their disability. It is expected that this will bring (critics say 'force') more disabled people into work and so make considerable savings.

Housing benefit

Housing benefit is being reformed. Effectively there is to be a cap on the benefit which means that an individual or family will only be able to claim benefit for rooms in their dwelling which are necessary according to the size of the family, essentially one bedroom per person or couple. If a family has 'spare' rooms, its benefit will be cut accordingly. Critics have called this the 'bedroom tax'.

Child benefit

Child benefit will be limited for wealthier families. If one or more parents in the family earns at least £60,000 per annum, no child benefit will be paid. If a parent earns between £50,000 and £60,000 per annum, child benefits will be progressively reduced. This applies from 2013 onwards.

Benefit fraud penalties

These are being substantially increased.

How much will be saved?

There is no certain figure specifying how much will be saved as a result of the reforms. However, the Institute of Fiscal Studies, an independent body, estimates that the saving in the financial year 2014/15, when the full effects of the changes will be first felt, will be £18 billion per year.

To place this in context, total expenditure on welfare benefits in that year is estimated at £214 billion. This means the reforms are estimated to save 8.3% of the total benefits budget. If we ignore expenditure on pensions, the saving is about 15%.

In the same year, 2014/15, it is expected (according to the independent Office for Budget Responsibility) that the government deficit will be £108 billion. Without the estimated benefit saving the deficit would be £126 billion. Therefore, the saving in benefits is estimated at 14% of the deficit in 1 year.

We can now summarise the financial significance of the changes in the year 2014/15:

- The saving on expenditure on benefits will be £18 billion.
- This saving amounts to 8.3% of the total benefits budget and 15% of the non-pension benefit budget.
- The saving represents an annual 14% reduction in the government deficit.

Why are the reforms being made?

Welfare reform is a central plank of the coalition government's platform. We can identify a number of reasons why such an ambitious programme is being implemented:

- There is a general public demand for reforms. It is a widely held view that too many people have entered what is known as a 'dependency culture' (a phrase initiated in the 1980s when Margaret Thatcher was prime minister). This suggests that there is a substantial minority who prefer to rely on state benefits than to earn their living independently. The main groups who have fallen under 'suspicion' are the unemployed — especially the young unemployed — the long-term sick and some who are claiming disability benefits. Many pressure groups argue that this is an exaggerated view, but the government is undoubtedly responding to the public and media mood on the issue.
- It may be the case — and government ministers believe — that the persistence of long-term unemployment is because it is too easy to claim benefits and many feel they are better off on benefits than in low-paid employment.
- The social security budget is a huge part of total public expenditure. If the government can make significant cuts (and all the reforms will save money) it will help it to reduce public expenditure and therefore the government deficit.

What do Labour and the Liberal Democrats say?

Table 4.1 shows which of the coalition policies the Labour Party agrees with and would retain if it came to power, alongside its own policy initiatives that differ from those of the coalition.

Table 4.1 Labour's attitude to welfare reform (announced by Ed Miliband, June 2013)

Areas of agreement	Areas of conflict and disagreement
• Labour would retain the idea of an overall cap on the total benefits a family can receive, though it may disagree on the level of the cap in the future. • Miliband accepts the idea of Personal Independence Payments (PIPs) for the disabled. There may be disagreement over detail and implementation. • As pensions are a major factor in the overall benefits bill, Labour accepts the need to raise the retirement age so that people will claim the state pension later in life, thus saving on the pensions bill. • Labour would support the removal of the Winter Fuel Allowance from wealthier pensioners. This is not yet proposed but is likely. • Labour would not restore child benefit to middle- and high-income families.	• Labour believes the welfare reforms are a short-term solution. The long-term solution to excessive benefits expenditure is a reduction in unemployment, especially long-term unemployment. • Labour would consider subsidising the employment of those who have been unemployed for over a year. This would mean paying employers to employ such people. The Conservatives oppose such 'job creation' schemes or interfering in labour markets. • Labour would increase the availability of nursery places for very young children to encourage young parents into work and so reduce the burden on benefits. • The Conservatives do not believe in interfering in labour markets but Labour embraces the concept of the 'living wage' that is higher than the minimum wage. It proposes that those who work for the state should be paid the living wage at least and would somehow persuade private employers to do likewise by offering tax cuts to those who do. This would reduce the need for benefits to top up low wages. • To reduce the housing benefit bill Labour is committed to building more houses and to encouraging this through state investment, rather than leaving it to market forces.

Though the right-hand column of Table 4.1 looks more substantial than the left, there is a considerable area of agreement over principles. In particular the agreement on the need for an overall benefits cap, the treatment of the disabled and the arrangements for child benefit are very similar. The main distinction lies in the way in which Labour would try to tackle unemployment and so bring down the expenditure on benefits.

Liberal Democrats are, of course, in government with the Conservatives and have therefore supported all the changes described above. They have, however, claimed

that there are differences in policy between the two parties and that they have had a decisive influence on policy so far. Three areas of difference between the coalition partners can be identified:

1 The Conservatives originally proposed that child benefit should not be paid for more than two children in a family. Liberal Democrats successfully opposed this.

2 The Conservative work and pensions secretary, Iain Duncan Smith, wanted to cut housing benefits for those under 25 (effectively more of them to live with parents). This was opposed as it might increase homelessness and encourage poverty among the young. It has been postponed, but remains Conservative party policy for the future.

3 Conservatives had hoped to reduce benefits expenditure by ensuring that the levels of benefit rose more slowly than the rate of inflation and the increase in tax rates. Liberal Democrats insisted that benefits should rise in line with prices.

Despite these areas of difference, as with Labour, there is a considerable level of agreement on benefits policy between the two coalition parties.

What is the deficit reduction plan?

The government hopes to have eliminated most of the government annual deficit by the end of the decade. The main ways in which this is to be achieved are as follows:

- There will be reductions in government expenditure almost across the board. Education and health, however, are to be exempt from such cuts.
- It is expected that there will be rising economic growth. When growth occurs there are two main effects on the deficit. First, the amount collected in taxes will automatically rise. Second, as unemployment and poverty fall, there will be less strain on the benefits bill.
- Some tax rates will rise, especially for those on middle-level incomes. (Tax rates on the poor will, however, continue to fall.)
- There is to be a concerted effort to reduce tax avoidance (legal) and evasion (illegal) and so increase tax revenues.

The key factor in this plan is economic growth. If the level of economic activity in the UK rises significantly in the next few years, the deficit will probably correct itself. If, however, economic growth is disappointing, the deficit is likely to persist.

Figure 4.1, produced by the independent Office for Budget Responsibility (OBR), indicates the official estimates of how reduction will progress in years to come.

We can see from Figure 4.1 that it is intended that the deficit, expressed as a percentage of GDP (that is, as a proportion of the total value of the economy's output), should fall to only 2.3% by 2018, down from its 2009 peak of 11.2% at the height of the financial crisis.

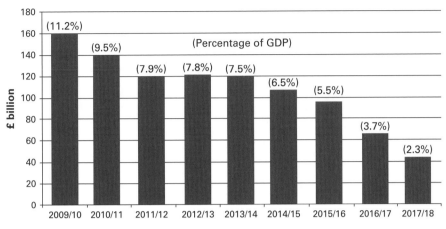

180
160
140
120
100
80
60
40
20
0

£ billion

(Percentage of GDP)

(11.2%)
(9.5%)
(7.9%) (7.8%) (7.5%)
(6.5%)
(5.5%)
(3.7%)
(2.3%)

2009/10 2010/11 2011/12 2012/13 2013/14 2014/15 2015/16 2016/17 2017/18

Figure 4.1 Public Sector Net Borrowing (PSNB, effectively the government 'deficit'), 2009–18

Source: OBR.

Note: This does not include government income from the sale of assets, such as the privatisation of Royal Mail in October 2013.

Summary

The title of this chapter questions whether the reforms to the welfare system of the UK are designed to improve society and the living conditions of its members, or are merely a means by which government costs can be cut and the public sector deficit reduced more quickly.

Certainly, the figures described above suggest that the reforms will have a major impact on deficit reduction (possibly as much as 15% of the reduction). Yet the fact that both the Labour and Liberal Democrat parties are in agreement with large parts of the programme suggests that there is a consensus for change that is genuine. In other words, the beneficial impact on government finances is a happy consequence rather than the driving force for change.

Labour continues to insist, however, that the long-term solution to the problem of the UK's enormous social security benefits bill lies with economic growth and the reduction in unemployment, rather than with tinkering with the social security system in the short term.

Exam focus

To consolidate your knowledge of this chapter, answer the following questions:

1 Why is welfare reform so important to the coalition government?
2 Why is the government deficit reduction plan so crucial?
3 Assess the effectiveness of the coalition's deficit reduction plan.
4 Explain the main controversies between the parties over welfare reform.

Chapter 5

Lobby and all-party groups: a threat to democracy?

Exam success

The up-to-date facts, examples and arguments in this chapter will help you to produce good-quality answers in your AS unit tests in the following areas of the specifications:

Edexcel	AQA	OCR
Unit 1	**Unit 1**	**Unit F851**
Pressure groups	Pressure groups and protest groups	Pressure groups

Context

There has recently been a growth in the number of lobby groups and so-called 'all-party groups' at Westminster. On the one hand, they mark nothing more than an extension in the scale of lobbying that is taking place, an inevitable development that is the result of increasing professionalism in pressure group activity; on the other, they are often criticised for being undemocratic.

This brief chapter explains what these groups are and then examines the extent to which they do represent a threat to an open democracy.

What are lobby groups?

Lobby groups are organised or semi-organised groups that lobby ministers and parliament on behalf of a section of society or in the pursuit of a particular cause. The term 'lobby' implies that they are insiders. The word itself stems from the open public area in the houses of parliament where members of the public have traditionally been able to meet with MPs and peers. Lobbying today means more than this. It means regular links with members of both houses of parliament, regular appearances before legislative and select committees as well as links with all-party groups that are discussed below. Lobby groups also seek to meet regularly with ministers, civil servants and official policy committees.

Concerns about the activities of such groups led to a campaign to set up a register of lobby groups in the UK (which exist in the European Parliament and the US Congress, for example). By the autumn of 2013 the government had finally responded to these demands and brought forward legislation (see below).

There are also a number of professional lobby groups, which are permanent organisations that use existing links with ministers, officials, advisers, MPs and peers to campaign on behalf of any group in return for substantial fees. In other words, there is now a small lobbying 'industry' in Westminster. They are, in theory, regulated by the Association of Professional Political Consultants (APPC), which seeks to control their conduct and maintain a register of responsible organisations, but this is only voluntary. These professional groups often employ former ministers, civil servants and MPs who have built up contacts during their political careers.

Examples of prominent 'insider' lobby groups include these:
- Campaign for Better Transport
- Campaign for Science and Engineering
- Migration Watch UK
- Age UK
- World Development Movement

What are all-party groups?

All-party groups are different to lobby groups. They number several hundred and all are kept on a register. Their members are MPs and peers, and some ministers may be members. They also sometimes employ paid research staff. They are divided into:
- **Country groups.** Virtually every country in the world is represented by an all-party group.
- **Subject groups.** These are concerned with a particular issue or cause.

Examples of subject groups include these:
- Consumer Affairs and Trading Standards
- Cycling
- Film Industry
- Malaria and Neglected Tropical Diseases
- Obesity
- Pensions
- Rugby League
- Sex Discrimination

The role of all-party groups remains rather vague and this gives cause for concern. Certainly, and harmlessly, they exist so that MPs and peers can become informed about countries and issues so as to improve their performance as legislators. However, they are also devices by which countries and lobby groups seek to influence MPs and peers.

Why are these groups controversial?

In February 2010, before he was elected prime minister and when he was leader of the opposition, Cameron made a speech criticising the lobby system at Whitehall. In it he said:

We all know how it works. The lunches, the hospitality, the quiet word in your ear, the ex-ministers and ex-advisors for hire, helping big business find the right way to get its way. In this party, we believe in competition, not cronyism. We believe in market economics, not crony capitalism. I believe that secret corporate lobbying, like the [MPs'] expenses scandal, goes to the heart of why people are so fed up with politics. It arouses people's worst fears and suspicions about how our political system works, with money buying power, power fishing for money and a cosy club at the top making decisions in their own interest.

Though Cameron was heavily critical of the system and predicted that it was 'the next big scandal to happen', and although reform of the lobby system was in the coalition agreement after the election, little has been done. There is a system to monitor the involvement of former ministers and civil servants in lobbying within 2 years of their leaving a job in government, but this is seen as largely ineffective. In September 2013, the government did produce draft legislation to create a register of lobby groups and lobbyists, but here again, critics say it will have little effect, as there are too few sanctions against those who would abuse the system.

Other than those mentioned in Cameron's remarks in 2010, there are a number of other criticisms of lobby groups:

- They are seen as channels of 'secret influence'.
- They may encourage corruption whereby MPs, peers and former ministers might enrich themselves by advising such groups and by offering to use their special contacts.
- There is a great danger that foreign states and companies may gain influence through the groups.
- Even if legislation is successfully passed in 2014, they are not regulated enough.

Box 5.1 The Lynton Crosby affair

Ironically, Cameron, who had warned about the dangers of lobbying in 2010, became personally involved in a potential lobbying scandal in November 2012 when he appointed an Australian consultant, Lynton Crosby, as the Conservatives' campaign manager.

The main problem is that Crosby runs a political consulting firm, Crosby Textor. This company includes among it clients private healthcare groups, the tobacco firm Philip Morris, and an Australian organisation involved in fracking. Charges have been made that Crosby may be using his position as election adviser to the Conservative Party, to lobby on behalf of his firm's clients. Specifically, this involves recent legislation or decisions on Health Service reform, regulation of cigarette marketing and taxes on fracking operations in the UK.

Crosby and Cameron deny any conflict of interests and insist that Crosby has not been lobbying on behalf of these and similar clients. Whether or not the charges are true, there is certainly an *appearance* of a conflict of interests.

A spokesman for the campaign group, Frack Off, said:

Crosby Textor and their clients are embedded at the heart of government. By smearing groups and communities that oppose shale oil and gas development they are simply trying to further their own financial interests and those of their clients.

In July 2013, Cameron, speaking on Andrew Marr's *Sunday Politics* show, said:

> Mr Crosby is advising the Conservative Party on how to take on Labour, how to make a political argument, how to prepare for the next campaign, but he's not advising us on policy or on issues...and he doesn't intervene in those.

The Transparency of Lobbying, Non-Party Campaigning and Trade Union Administration Bill 2013–14

Apart from having a tremendously cumbersome title, the bill to control lobbying is designed to do several things:

- To create a register of lobby groups. The implication of this is that if any lobby group misbehaves, it will be removed from the register and lose its privileges in Westminster.
- It demands that trade unions and other lobby groups keep proper and accurate records of their membership. This is designed to ensure that 'undesirable members' are eliminated from the lobbying process. A certification officer post will be appointed to check membership records and take action if they are not satisfactory.
- It regulates and limits election spending by lobby groups (i.e. funding for candidates by such groups). Groups will have a cap of £390,000 imposed on them for their total expenses on lobbying during elections.

At the end of 2013, this bill is in the House of Lords. Its passage had been difficult and will continue to be so, as many MPs and peers feel it is much too weak and too complicated.

Summary

Having established that the activities of lobby groups and all-party groups are causing concern, we need to evaluate whether they are doing harm to UK democracy.

The arguments that they represent **a threat to democracy** include these:

- All-party groups are not supposed to be lobby groups, but will be seeking influence for outside groups behind the scenes.
- All-party groups are able to issue passes allowing people to operate inside parliament and this is not properly regulated.
- Both all-party and lobby groups create opportunities for corrupt practices whereby MPs and peers may accept money in return for insider lobbying.
- Lobbying is a hidden form of influence. Lobby groups, whether they are professional or not, are not accountable and have been unregulated for many years.
- Lobbying is an expensive business and it may provide opportunities for wealthy countries and outside groups to be able to wield influence, using their wealth rather than the real value of their cause.

Democracy requires openness (transparency) and opportunities for all sections of society, not just wealthy ones, to be able to access the political system. It can be argued that lobby groups, in particular, threaten these principles.

Exam focus

To consolidate your knowledge of this chapter, answer the following questions:

1 Do insider pressure groups enhance or threaten democracy?
2 Explain how lobby groups are regulated at Westminster.
3 In what ways can it be said 'money matters' in pressure group politics?

Chapter 6

E-petitions: a form of democratic renewal?

Exam success

The up-to-date facts, examples and arguments in this chapter will help you to produce good-quality answers in your AS unit tests in the following areas of the specifications:

Edexcel	AQA	OCR
Unit 1 Democracy and political participation	**Unit 1** Participation	**Unit F851** Pressure groups

Context

An e-petition is a general name given to any petition that is conducted online. In theory, any individual may start such a petition but, in practice, it is most likely to be noticed if it is placed on an established e-petition site. There are many such sites, but three that have particular impact are:

- the Downing Street site: **http://epetitions.direct.gov.uk**
- the 38 Degrees campaign site: **www.38degrees.org.uk**
- the change.org site: **www.change.org**

In common with each other, these sites are easy to use, new petitions can be established very quickly, they are free and they have a high profile so they attract many visitors and participants.

The official government site (**http://epetitions.direct.gov.uk**) is potentially the most important as it can force government departments to review an issue and, in some cases, can trigger a debate in parliament.

At first sight, it may seem that the development of e-petitions is wholly beneficial to democracy, but this chapter also examines the extent to which they may not enhance democracy in all cases.

It should be noted that petitions of any kind are not, strictly speaking, forms of direct democracy, as they do not lead specifically to decision making. However, they can be seen as part of a new *consultative* and *participatory* form of democracy, which stands as a rival to representative democracy, alongside direct democracy (largely in the form of referendums) itself.

Current and recent e-petitions

Table 6.1 shows a number of petitions that have attracted considerable attention and may prove to have some impact. It is interesting to note that such petitions may cover all kinds of issues at different levels. The varying types are also shown in Table 6.1.

Table 6.1 Examples of current and recent e-petitions

Site	Campaign	Support level (up to December 2013)	Type
Downing Street	Full disclosure of all government documents relating to 1989 Hillsborough disaster.	Closed in August 2013. Attracted 156,216 signatures.	An issue largely related to Liverpool, but also of national concern.
Downing Street	Stop the Badger Cull. Against the culling of badgers to prevent the spread of bovine tuberculosis.	Closed in September 2013. Attracted 304,148 signatures (the cull went ahead).	National issue.
Downing Street	Return Shaker Aamer to the UK. Aamer is the last British detainee held at Guantánamo Bay by the USA on suspicion of terrorism.	Closed in April 2013. Attracted 117,456 signatures.	National and international human rights issue.
38 Degrees	Ban the pesticides that are killing bees.	Current. In December 2013 it had attracted 330,127 signatures.	National issue.
38 Degrees	Stop the gas and electricity rip-off.	Current. In December 2013 it had attracted 103,431 signatures.	National issue.
Change.org	Oxfordshire Council: stop making people with learning disabilities homeless through budget cuts.	Current. In December 2013 it had attracted 144,489 signatures.	A local issue with national implications.
Change.org	Pembrokeshire Council: grant retrospective planning permission to Charlie and Meg's roundhouse.	Current. In December 2013 it had attracted 88,056 signatures.	A local and personal petition.

We can see from Table 5.1 that e-petitions now cover a wide variety of issues, which may be local, regional or national (or indeed international). They may be of general concern, or only related to a section of society, or even to a single individual. One of the virtues of e-petitions is that they can cover all these kinds of issues without any section of society having an advantage over any other. They disperse influence and participation.

Box 6.1 **The Hillsborough disaster and its aftermath**

The role of an e-petition in the campaign for justice for the victims of the Hillsborough disaster is perhaps the best example of the potential impact of such devices.

On 15 April 1996, 96 people were killed and 766 injured at Hillsborough football ground in Sheffield at the start of an FA Cup semi-final between Liverpool and Nottingham Forest. Most of the victims were from Liverpool. A section of the ground became dangerously overcrowded when police let a large number of people into a confined space on the terraces. The resulting crush caused the casualties. The police who were on duty reported that most of the blame lay with the supporters themselves, and the press also suggested that bad behaviour by Liverpool supporters was the cause. Since then there has been a sustained campaign among those connected with the victims to prove that the fault lay with the police and that, furthermore, the police had concealed and/or falsified their own record of the events. The focus of the campaign lay with the missing police records.

When Downing Street opened its e-petition site, a campaign for signatures was initiated by the Hillsborough campaigners. Nearly 140,000 people signed up, requesting the publication of all police records. The petition triggered a parliamentary debate, and the House of Commons passed a motion ordering full publication of the records. As a result, it has been revealed that there is a case for suggesting the police were at fault and, more seriously, that many of their statements were probably false. The issue is ongoing, but the campaigners now have most of the information they need to pursue their case for justice.

Without the e-petition this issue may not have been debated, and it is probable that most of the relevant information would have been suppressed.

Further examples of debates triggered by e-petitions have been:
- **2012:** the proposed reforms to the NHS
- **2012:** the granting of a new franchise for the West Coast main railway line
- **2013:** Shaker Aamer (see Table 6.1)

Are e-petitions good for democracy?

On the face of it such petitions must be good for democracy, but a full evaluation needs to be considered before we rush to judgement.

Positive aspects of e-petitions
- Clearly, they enable many people to participate in the democratic process, many of whom would not normally take part.

- In that sense they help to disperse influence (pluralism) and reduce the accumulation of influence in too few hands (elitism).
- They are a cheap, easy way in which campaigners can gain some access to decision makers.
- They are a cheap and efficient way for pressure groups to mobilise public opinion.
- They are peaceful and not disruptive to society in any way.
- They are a useful way for government itself to gauge public opinion on certain issues.
- In a few cases they may result in change through the democratic process.

Negative aspects of e-petitions

- They do not necessarily reflect the will of the majority, only those who take the trouble to participate. They may, therefore, give a false view of public opinion.
- They may begin to undermine the system of representative democracy where the interests of minorities are balanced against each other, or against that of the majority, by elected, accountable representatives. This is a general criticism of any form of direct democracy.
- The actual wording of such petitions may be misleading and lead to a particular conclusion.
- Many issues are too complex to be resolved by a simple demand in a petition.
- E-petitions may be hacked or corrupted by vested interests and so give a false picture of how much support an issue actually has.

Summary

The impact of e-petitions is difficult to assess. We can say that there is little *concrete evidence* that they change decision making. The Hillsborough case, described above, is a rare example of a *specific* impact. However, they may well have an effect that is less tangible. They can certainly place issues on the political agenda, which might otherwise disappear. They also play a part in what is known as *tension release*. This implies that citizens feel they can air their grievances in public and possibly in parliament. They probably fall short of representing 'democratic renewal' but they do have a positive effect on political participation and the dispersal of information to the citizenry.

Exam focus

To consolidate your knowledge of this chapter, answer the following questions:

1 Assess the effectiveness of e-petitions in promoting political participation.
2 Examine the problems created by the use of e-petitions.
3 What is meant by the term 'consultative democracy'?
4 Examine the case for the further use of e-petitions in the governing process.

Chapter 7

Boris Johnson: Britain's next Conservative prime minister?

Exam success

The up-to-date facts, examples and arguments in this chapter will help you to produce good-quality answers in your AS unit tests in the following areas of the specifications:

Edexcel	AQA	OCR
Unit 1 Political parties	**Unit 1** Political parties	**Unit F851** Political parties
Unit 2 Prime minister and cabinet	**Unit 2** The core executive	**Unit F852** The executive

Context

Boris Johnson comes from what can be described as a 'political dynasty'. These are quite common in politics. Ed Miliband's father, Ralph, was a political activist and his brother was a Labour minister. John Cryer is a current Labour MP whose father, Bob, and mother, Ann, were also prominent MPs. The son of former prime minister, Harold Macmillan (1957–63), Maurice, was a government minister and his grandson was an MEP. In Johnson's case his father, Stanley, is a long-time Conservative Party activist and a former MEP and parliamentary candidate. His brother, Joe, is an MP and his sister, Rachel, a political journalist.

A biography of Boris Johnson looks like this:

Born: 1964 in the USA of English parents.
Educated: Brussels European School, Eton and Oxford.
Occupation: Journalist on the *Telegraph*, *The Times* and *Spectator* magazine (the latter as editor).
2001–08: Conservative MP for Henley on Thames.
2008: Elected London Mayor, defeating Ken Livingstone.
2012: Re-elected London Mayor, defeating Livingstone again.

Up to 2008, when he became London mayor, Johnson's *curriculum vitae* looks typically that of a future prime minister. However, Johnson is far from typical for two reasons. First, there is his experience of running London for several years. As this position only came into existence recently, it is not 'normal' experience for a political leader. (In France, on the other hand, it is common for ministers, prime ministers and even presidents to be former mayors of large cities.) Second, Johnson is seen as something of an unconventional Conservative thinker, often described as a 'maverick'.

Boris Johnson's political beliefs

Johnson expresses an unusual mixture of ideas taken from three different traditions. These are summarised below in Table 7.1.

Table 7.1 Boris Johnson's political beliefs summarised

'Thatcherite' ideas	'Mainstream, centre' ideas	Liberal ideas	Other unclassified views
• Direct taxes on income should be as low as possible, especially on businesses. • Governments should interfere as little as possible in the working of markets and the economy. • Johnson takes a hard line on preventing abuse of the benefits system, believing in the dangers of a 'dependency culture'. • He takes a hard line, zero-tolerance approach to crime and punishment. • He supports a very free financial market system with open access to London.	• Johnson is a Eurosceptic but only mildly, and believes the UK should stay in the EU on renegotiated terms. • He supports the Gove reforms of examinations on the whole, and supports wide choice in types of schooling available. • He supports orthodox, Conservative welfare reform. • He opposes the 'rights culture' and would replace the ECHR with a British Bill of Rights.	• Johnson supports gay marriage. • He takes a liberal view of abortion. • He is not hard line on immigration and sees it largely as a positive phenomenon. He proposes an amnesty for long-stay illegal immigrants. • He takes a liberal view of multiculturalism, believing that ethnic and cultural diversity enrich society.	• There should be a new airport for London. • The rise in house prices should be tackled by building more houses. • He would like to abolish stamp duty on house purchases. • He supports HS2.

So we can see that Johnson does not fit neatly into any one political tradition. In summary, he is a social liberal who holds neo-liberal, right-wing economic views. On most issues he professes to support Cameron and the government, but there remains some doubt as to how loyal he really is to the Conservative leadership.

Johnson's performance as London Mayor

As usual in politics, any assessment of Johnson's performance as mayor is mixed. To some extent this depends on the observer's own political allegiance, but it is possible to make a neutral evaluation. Table 7.2 offers such an assessment. It should be noted that opinions often differ about his so-called achievements or failures. Where there are serious disputes about performance, they are shown in the table.

Table 7.2 An assessment of Boris Johnson's performance as London Mayor

Commonly perceived successes	Commonly perceived failures
• The Olympics and Paralympics were viewed as great successes. Johnson was supportive and seen as a major asset (shared with Ken Livingstone). • Most agree that London transport, especially buses, has improved greatly. Some dispute that the London Underground has improved but it is now very expensive. • It appears that the Crossrail project is likely to be delivered on time and within budget. • There have been significant falls in most crimes in London in recent years, despite falling police numbers. • Under both Johnson and Livingstone, the London economy has grown, especially the financial sector (though many argue there is insufficient regulation). • He has successfully encouraged a growth in cycling in London (some say it is inadequate) and introduced 'Boris bikes' for general use, free for short journeys.	• He has not solved the problem of airport capacity in London. • There has been considerable unrest among the emergency services over closures, staff reductions and worsening working conditions. • There remains a chronic shortage of affordable housing in London. • There have been a number of 'financial scandals' involving senior staff, including the resignation of Ray Lewis shortly after his appointment as assistant mayor for young people. Johnson's judgement on appointments is often questioned. • There remain pockets of high unemployment — especially among the young — in London (though many say this is outside his political control and is a national issue).

This assessment represents a fairly balanced picture. Johnson still has at least 3 more years in office before he needs to seek re-election, so there is time for more successes or failures before the issue of the Conservative leadership is likely to come up. Both his supporters and opponents will be able to find plenty of ammunition from his time as mayor.

The Conservative succession — scenarios

What has to happen if Boris Johnson is to become prime minister? The answer is: a great deal. Here are the possible scenarios.

Scenario 1

The Conservative Party continues to lie behind Labour in the opinion polls and also faces some challenges from UKIP. The party, especially its right-wing elements, decide that Cameron is the problem, notably because he is too 'moderate'. There is a coup d'état in the party, of the kind that ousted Thatcher in 1990. In a leadership election, Johnson wins. This causes a problem as he is not an MP and, by convention, prime ministers must also be MPs. Johnson would have to be found a safe seat very quickly (i.e. a willing Conservative MP would stand down and there would be a by-election). There is a precedent for this. In 1963, prime minister Harold Macmillan stood down through ill health and Lord Home, a Tory peer, was chosen to replace him. In order to follow the convention, he had to be found a safe seat to contest. Home renounced his peerage, fought a by-election, and became an MP and then prime minister.

Scenario 2

Cameron resigns suddenly for some reason such as ill health, family issues, a scandal or the like. Harold Macmillan in 1963, Harold Wilson in 1976, and Tony Blair in 2007 all resigned while in office for various reasons. In each case their party held a leadership election to find the new prime minister. Here again, Johnson would need a safe seat to put him in the House of Commons.

Scenario 3

If the Conservatives lose the 2015 election they may well wish to dispense with Cameron as their leader or he may resign. By then, Johnson could have become an MP. Even if he has not, he could be elected leader and would have plenty of time to find a parliamentary seat before the next election. Of course, the Conservatives would then have to win that election.

Scenario 4

The Conservatives win the 2015 general election, Cameron carries on for a while and then decides to resign before the following election. Johnson by then may well be an MP and be in pole position to take over. As things stand this looks like the most likely scenario.

So, as we can see, the road to No. 10 would not be an easy one for Boris Johnson. There are many ifs and buts along the way.

How secure is Cameron?

All this depends on how secure Cameron's position is as Conservative leader and prime minister. If he remains leader, wins the 2015 general election and serves another full term, Johnson will probably have missed his chance for good. But is Cameron in any immediate danger of losing the Conservative leadership? We will now examine this issue.

Positives for Cameron

- The British economy is recovering as Cameron promised it would. Unemployment and crime rates are falling, interest rates are low and inflation remains under control.
- Despite the recession and the austerity that followed, the Labour lead over the Conservatives is not widening and is modest enough to give the Conservatives hope of closing the gap.
- There is no obvious successor to Cameron (other than Johnson, perhaps, and he is not an MP as was pointed out above).
- Ed Miliband is making relatively little impact.

Negatives for Cameron

- The odds remain stacked against a Conservative outright victory in 2015. The Conservative Party usually gets rid of leaders who do not deliver election victories. Since 1997, the party has dispensed with four leaders — Major, Hague, Duncan Smith and Howard.
- Cameron is constantly threatened by powerful right-wing, Eurosceptic elements in his own party. He is seen by them as being too weak and moderate.
- Boris Johnson is now beginning to emerge as a credible alternative to him.

Box 7.1 How popular is Boris Johnson?

YouGov, a polling organisation, carried out a survey of voters in January 2013, comparing attitudes to the performance of various political leaders. The result was startling. The question asked whether respondents thought each leader was doing a good job or not. The results came out in the form of net approval or net disapproval ratings. All the leaders had negative ratings except one — Boris Johnson. These were the figures:

Boris Johnson	+53%
Ed Miliband	−13%
David Cameron	−19%
George Osborne	−30%
Nick Clegg	−44%

Source: YouGov.

Political leadership in Britain

What does it take to be a successful political leader in Britain? If we can answer this question, we will understand more about Boris Johnson's future prospects. A summary of the necessary leadership qualities includes those shown below. You may wish to think about how many of these boxes Johnson ticks. The summary that follows offers some additional suggestions.

- Clearly, he/she must enjoy some public popularity. Ed Miliband is often seen as an unsatisfactory leader because he lacks this quality.
- He/she must have a power base in his/her own party, i.e. a sizeable number of supporters who will help him/her get elected as leader and will act as a loyal team to consolidate his/her leadership.

- He/she should have no serious 'skeletons' in the cupboard, such as personal scandals or serious errors of judgement made in the past.
- He/she needs relevant experience. This often means service in local councils and as an MP or MEP. Increasingly it means working for the party in some capacity. Past occupation(s) have become less important.
- He/she should be able to cope with the rough and tumble of parliament, especially at question time and during controversial debates.
- He/she needs a good media image.

Box 7.2 Was he really joking?

In September 2013 Johnson addressed the Conservative Party annual conference. At one point he seemed to be opening up the idea that a city mayor could be prime minister at the same time. But was he, as he claimed, only joking? Here is the relevant extract:

> ...not so long ago I welcomed the former French Prime Minister, Monsieur Alain Juppe to my office in City Hall and he cruised in with his sizeable retinue of very distinguished fellows with their legion d'honneur floret and all the rest of it and we shook hands and had a tête a tête and he told me that he was now the Mayor of Bordeaux. I think he may have been Mayor of Bordeaux when he was Prime Minister, it's the kind of thing they do in France — a very good idea in my view. Joke, joke, joke!

Summary

As we have seen, a number of events must occur if Boris Johnson is to become a future Conservative leader and possible prime minister. If we assume the circumstances are 'favourable' to his prospects, his strengths and weaknesses as a future prime minister are summarised in Table 7.3.

Table 7.3 Boris Johnson's prime ministerial credentials

Strengths	Weaknesses
■ He is a popular politician, considered to be charismatic and entertaining. He breaks the mould of 'machine politicians' who have little experience of life outside the Westminster bubble. ■ He has, arguably, a good track record as London Mayor. He is also, therefore, experienced in running a large political unit. ■ His breadth of political beliefs may appeal to a wide section of the electorate.	■ He is prone to gaffes, in particular insulting various sections of British society. ■ He has a 'colourful' private life, with rumours of extra-marital affairs and even children outside his marriages (for some, his interesting personality may be a strength, of course). ■ He does not have a 'power base' within the Conservative Party. He has been out of Westminster politics for several years. ■ It may be that his lack of a recognisable political ideology confuses party members and voters.

Exam focus

To consolidate your knowledge of this chapter, answer the following questions:

1 Explain how a politician can become prime minister.
2 How important a political role is that of London Mayor?
3 What do Boris Johnson's political beliefs tell us about the divisions within the Conservative Party?

Chapter 8

Select committees: are they effective?

Exam success

The up-to-date facts, examples and arguments in this chapter will help you to produce good-quality answers in your AS unit tests in the following areas of the specifications:

Edexcel	AQA	OCR
Unit 2	**Unit 2**	**Unit F852**
Parliament	Parliament	The legislature

Context

Both houses of parliament contain many committees, which are described as 'select'. However, for the purposes of this Annual Update and any examination questions you may face, we need only consider two types of committee. These are **departmental select committees**, which were founded in 1979, and the **Public Accounts Committee** (PAC), which is parliament's longest-standing select committee, dating back to 1861.

Despite the name 'select', which suggests they may have a temporary membership, the committees are actually permanent during the life of a parliament. Members, therefore, can expect to remain on the committee for that period at least.

The role of the Public Accounts Committee (PAC)

The easiest way to begin a description of the role of the PAC is to quote directly from its terms of reference as described on the UK Parliament website:

> The Committee of Public Accounts is appointed by the House of Commons to examine 'the accounts showing the appropriation of the sums granted to Parliament to meet the public expenditure, and of such other accounts laid before Parliament as the Committee may think fit'.

> The Committee does **not** consider the formulation or merits of policy (which fall within the scope of departmental select committees); rather it focuses on value-for-money criteria which are based on economy, effectiveness and efficiency.
>
> Source: www.parliament.uk

Note that the committee does not examine government policy, but the ways in which government revenues are raised and spent. It also looks at public bodies such as the BBC (because parliament approves the licence fee) and various agencies of the state that are funded by government such as the NHS. In effect, therefore, the committee is looking after the interests of citizens as taxpayers. Two fundamental questions are asked by the PAC:

- Are taxes being raised efficiently and effectively?
- Is government achieving 'value for money' in its spending?

It should therefore be noted that the committee does not concern itself with how public money is allocated (i.e. how much is spent on health, or education or defence and so on). It also does not pass opinions on what kind of taxes are raised or how the tax burden is distributed.

The membership of the PAC

It is most important to note that the chair of the committee is always, by tradition, a prominent member of the main opposition party. This is symbolic of the committee's independence. The position is much sought after as it carries a great deal of political prestige and an addition to the MP's salary.

The rest of the committee is made up of backbench MPs (ministers are never members), in rough proportion to the representation of the parties in the whole House of Commons. In 2013 the party balance of the committee was as follows:

Conservative	8
Labour	5 (including Margaret Hodge, Chair)
Liberal Democrat	1

The chair of the PAC is elected by all MPs and the members are elected by MPs of their own party. This helps to maintain their independence from the party whips and leaderships.

Procedures and powers

The committee has powers to call witnesses. These may be anyone they feel can help, including ministers, civil servants and any other persons involved in taxation or public expenditure. They may also call for official papers and any other evidence they want. The only exceptions to this are members of the royal family or any evidence, either verbal or written, which might compromise national security. The proceedings of the committee are televised so there is maximum publicity. Questioning by the committee can be notoriously robust and witnesses may find themselves cross-examined very much as they might be in a court of law.

The committee does not have the power to change government policy or to recommend punishments for wrongdoers. All it can do is to produce reports to parliament as a whole. These reports may recommend action, but the committee has no way of enforcing such reports. Only Parliament can order specific actions.

Prominent recent investigations by the PAC

Table 8.1 shows some recent prominent investigations and reports by the PAC.

Table 8.1 Recent prominent investigations and reports by the PAC

Investigation	Report	Recommendation(s) and effect
Rural broadband contracts, September 2013	The PAC took the view that the government's programme of providing broadband internet connections to rural areas was over-generous to BT, which was awarded nearly all the contracts. It also suggested that the lack of competition for contracts meant that too much was being paid for broadband.	The PAC recommended that the government should not offer any more broadband contracts until it had ensured there would be more competition between providers. The government rejected the charges but there was widespread media criticism of the programme.
Google's alleged tax avoidance scheme, June 2013	The PAC criticised Her Majesty's Revenue and Customs (HMRC) for failing to collect enough tax due from Google's UK operations.	HMRC agreed that it would re-examine Google's affairs.
The decision to go ahead with the High Speed 2 (HS2) scheme for fast train services to Birmingham and the north, September 2013	The PAC criticised the plans, arguing that the costs were excessive and there was no guarantee it would not cost considerably more. It also suggested that the case for HS2 was probably not strong enough, given its very high cost.	The Labour Party decided to reassess its own support for the project. Many MPs, including some Conservatives, called for the project to be abandoned or reduced.

The role of departmental select committees

Unlike the PAC, the departmental select committees do look at government policies and make comments on their desirability. Each committee 'shadows' a government department, constantly monitoring its work. It should be noted that the PAC (see above) can also look at the way in which some government departments manage their financial affairs.

The kind of issues that these committees investigate are:

- How desirable and effective are the policies of the department?
- Does the department provide 'value for money'?

- Has the department dealt fairly and effectively with the public?
- If there has been a major issue arising within the department's responsibilities, the committee can investigate how well or badly it was dealt with by ministers and officials.
- How well is the department managed?

The committees and their membership

Members of the committees, who are all backbench MPs (i.e. not ministers or shadow ministers), are chosen by MPs of their own parties. The chairs are also chosen by MPs. Most chairs are from the governing party or parties, but not all. The membership of a committee is drawn from parties roughly in proportion to the strength of the parties in the House of Commons as a whole. Members of the committees are expected to behave in an independent way and should not be put under pressure to behave in a certain way by the party whips. The departmental select committees vary in size from 11 to 14 members. They have a small staff of researchers to help them.

Table 8.2 shows the departmental select committees in session as of October 2013. This demonstrates how independent the committees can be. Several have Labour or Liberal Democrat chairs, smaller parties have some members, and no single party has a majority on any committee.

Table 8.2 Departmental select committees in session as of October 2013

Committee	Chair's party	Membership make-up
Business, Innovation and Skills	Labour	5 Conservative, 5 Labour, 1 Liberal Democrat
Communities and Local Government	Labour	5 Conservative, 5 Labour, 1 Liberal Democrat
Culture, Media and Sport	Conservative	5 Conservative, 5 Labour, 1 Liberal Democrat
Defence	Conservative	5 Conservative, 5 Labour, 1 Liberal Democrat, 1 Democratic Unionist (Northern Ireland)
Education	Conservative	5 Conservative, 5 Labour, 1 Independent
Energy and Climate Change	Conservative	5 Conservative, 5 Labour, 1 Liberal Democrat
Environment, Food and Rural Affairs	Conservative	5 Conservative, 4 Labour, 1 Liberal Democrat, 1 SDLP (Northern Ireland)
Foreign Affairs	Conservative	5 Conservative, 5 Labour, 1 Liberal Democrat
Health	Conservative	5 Conservative, 5 Labour, 1 Liberal Democrat

Committee	Chair's party	Membership make-up
Home Affairs	Labour	5 Conservative, 5 Labour, 1 Liberal Democrat
International Development	Liberal Democrat	5 Conservative, 5 Labour, 1 Liberal Democrat
Justice	Liberal Democrat	5 Conservative, 5 Labour, 1 Liberal Democrat, 1 Plaid Cymru
Northern Ireland	Conservative	5 Conservative, 4 Labour, 1 Independent, 2 Democratic Unionist (NI), 1 Alliance (NI), 1 SDLP (NI)
Scottish	Labour	5 Labour, 3 Conservative, 2 Liberal Democrat, 1 Scottish National Party
Transport	Labour	5 Conservative, 5 Labour, 1 Liberal Democrat
Treasury	Conservative	6 Conservative, 5 Labour, 1 Liberal Democrat, 1 Scottish National Party
Welsh	Conservative	5 Conservative, 5 Labour, 1 Liberal Democrat, 1 Plaid Cymru
Work and Pensions	Labour	5 Conservative, 5 Labour, 1 Liberal Democrat

Procedures and powers

The powers and procedures of these committees are very similar to those of the PAC. They have the same powers as law courts to call witnesses and may ask for official papers. Their questioning of ministers, civil servants and officials can be aggressive and witnesses are not permitted to refuse to answer questions.

At the end of an investigation and in each parliamentary session, the committees produce reports to the rest of Parliament, assessing the performance of the department and making judgements on specific issues. They may recommend changes of decision or policies and may also simply criticise. However, like the PAC they cannot enforce their recommendations.

As far as possible, the committees produce unanimous reports as they carry more cross-party authority. Where this is not possible they produce two reports, one supported by the majority, the other by a minority.

Prominent recent investigations by departmental select committees

Table 8.3 shows some recent prominent investigations and reports by departmental select committees.

Table 8.3 Prominent investigations and reports by departmental select committees

Committee	Investigation	Report	Recommendation(s) and effect
Education	The legacy of the London 2012 Olympics in school sport, July 2013.	The committee was critical of a failure of government to follow up the Olympic legacy by adopting long-term (rather than the current 2-year) funding for increased school sport.	Little impact on government, but Labour made a stronger future commitment to encouraging school sport to follow up the Olympic legacy.
Environment, Food and Rural Affairs	An inquiry into the government's proposed legislation to stiffen action against dangerous dogs, May 2013.	The committee argued that the proposed legislation did not go far enough, especially in relation to 'out-of-control' dogs.	The government agreed to add amendments to the legislation to address the committee's concerns.
Home affairs	The growth of online crime in Britain, July 2013.	The committee expressed great concern that not enough was being done to combat increasing 'cyber crime', such as online fraud.	The government gave assurances that the new National Crime Agency (NCA), launched in October 2013, would have a dedicated unit with large numbers of experts working on the problem.

The influence of select committees

Much of the influence of departmental select committees is hidden. In other words, we cannot necessarily see the effects of their investigations but they have certainly had some impact. Their influence has the following aspects:

■ Most importantly, departmental select committees make government accountable. The other channels of accountability, notably parliamentary debates, minister's question days and Prime Minister's Questions are much less effective. The whips head off serious criticisms and ministers are skilled at avoiding difficult examination. The select committees, however, are much less suppressed by party whips and are more independent minded. The chairs (who receive an additional salary) tend to be unaffected by the patronage of their party leaders.

■ They may have a significant effect on governance. This implies that decision-makers and policy-makers have to take into account the fact that what they

do is likely to be closely scrutinised by the committees. They therefore have to ensure that what they decide will be effective, value for money and fair to those whom their decisions affect. So, since 1979, we could argue that the committees have improved the quality of government.

- They can place important issues on the political agenda, often issues that government might like to bury. In 2013, for example, various committees have thrown light on such problems as the management of the BBC, the desirability or otherwise of fracking for gas, whether High Speed 2 is value for money, what to do about press regulation and how to regulate the banks.

The weaknesses of select committees

The committees have a number of significant weaknesses. Among them are the following:

- Above all, they cannot enforce their recommendations. They have no powers over legislation, they cannot order dismissals of ministers, officials or advisers, and they cannot order compensation to be paid to wronged persons (though they can make strong recommendations).
- They only have small research staffs and so have some difficulty in making investigations because MPs have insufficient time or means to do so.
- Although over a period of years the members build up knowledge and expertise, they do not have the same knowledge of their subject as many of the witnesses.
- Although their proceedings are reported and often televised, they lack publicity. Where a major issue of public interest is concerned, they do gain publicity, but much of their work is buried, thus reducing their impact.

Summary

One additional aspect of these committees should be emphasised. Under coalition none of the committees contains a majority of MPs from one single party. This reflects the fact that there is a hung parliament. It is, therefore, much less likely that the government and its whips can put pressure on their own members to produce favourable reports. In other words, since 2010, the committees have shown much greater independence.

The work of the PAC and some of the departmental select committees burst into prominence during 2013. In particular **Margaret Hodge**, the feisty chair of the PAC, has become a major public figure. Hodge is a former Labour minister and ex-leader of Islington Council and so has great political experience. Her robust questioning of such witnesses as leading civil servants in her Majesty's Revenue and Customs (over tax evasion and avoidance), the management of the BBC (over excessive salaries and payoffs for senior executives) and transport ministers (over the growing cost and delay of High Speed 2) has brought her to prominence. Many argue that she is now as important a politician as any individual government minister.

That said, the committees are still hampered by the weaknesses described above. We can therefore say that they have been effective in three main ways and also continue to be weak in three ways. These are summarised in Table 8.4.

Table 8.4 Assessment of House of Commons select committees

Positive aspects of effectiveness emerging in 2013	Remaining weaknesses
1 Some committees have achieved great publicity over a number of issues and raised important political debates. 2 Some committee members and chairs have become key political figures. 3 Select committees are increasingly making parliament more effective in calling government to account. This is particularly true under coalition where no party has a majority on any committee.	1 They still cannot enforce their decisions. 2 Much of the work of committees is scarcely noticed by the public or the media and so their impact is minimal. 3 Many members still lack the knowledge, expertise or research back-up to be effective.

Exam focus

To consolidate your knowledge of this chapter, answer the following questions:

1 Explain the powers of select committees.
2 Explain the weaknesses of select committees.
3 Why is the PAC so influential?
4 What are the main distinctions between parliamentary select committees and legislative committees?
5 How important are parliamentary select committees?

Chapter 9

'Civil servants advise, ministers decide': fact or fiction?

Exam success

The up-to-date facts, examples and arguments in this chapter will help you to produce good-quality answers in your AS unit tests in the following areas of the specifications:

Edexcel	AQA	OCR
Unit 2	**Unit 2**	**Unit F852**
Prime minister and cabinet	The core executive	The executive

Context

The expression 'Civil servants advise, ministers decide' is a precise way of describing the relationship between elected politicians and unelected civil servants. It carries a world of meaning. In essence it is expected that civil servants may give advice to ministers, but only on the following basis:

- The advice must be neutral.
- It must not guide the minister towards a particular decision.
- It will give the minister the full range of options available to him/her.
- It will point out the advantages and disadvantages of each option in a balanced way.

Ministers, on the other hand, *are* expected to make decisions. Ministers are accountable and therefore must accept responsibility for such decisions.

In reality, however, the truth may be rather more blurred. In addition, the picture has become increasingly confused by the growth in the use of special political advisers by ministers. There is now less of a distinction between civil servants and advisers than ever before. This chapter examines some of the evidence as to whether the traditional relationship between ministers and civil servants is still relevant.

The traditional position of civil servants

Civil servants are expected to have three characteristics. These have been so fixed that they are often said to be constitutional principles. They are as follows:

1 **They are neutral.** This means that the advice they give must be free from any bias towards the fortunes of one political party or another. Civil servants serve

the state, not the ruling party. This also implies that, when the government changes from one party to another, they should serve their new political masters with the same degree of professionalism as the previous ones. Senior civil servants are not permitted to engage in active party politics.

2 **They are permanent.** All this means is that civil servants remain in their post even when the government changes. Of course, individuals will move departments and be promoted from time to time, but it is an important principle that an incoming government must accept the civil servants whom it inherits. Note that this is in contrast to the United States where a new senior civil service is recruited when a new president comes to office.

3 **They must be anonymous.** This means two things. First, their precise role in government should not be revealed. This does not mean their name and rank and department are not known, simply that the work they are doing is confidential. This is to prevent them being put under pressure from outside forces. Second, it means that they cannot be made publicly accountable for what they do. Instead, their minister must make him/herself responsible for what his/her department does. If civil servants were accountable it would expose them to outside pressure.

Ministers, on the other hand, are the opposite. They are certainly not permanent and may lose office at any time. Obviously, they are not neutral as they are leading members of their party, and they are far from anonymous so they can be made accountable for their actions and those of their department.

Private advisers also do not conform to the civil service principles described above. They give biased, political advice, they can be hired or fired by ministers at any time and their role is well known to the media and therefore the public.

Is this relationship changing?
In September 2013 Peter Riddell, a celebrated political commentator, wrote a report for the Institute for Government, which was presented to the Conservative Party conference. His main criticisms of the changing relationships were these:
- Civil servants are increasingly being openly questioned by departmental select committees in parliament and by the House of Commons Public Accounts Committee. This means their anonymity is destroyed and makes them accountable to parliament for their advice.
- Ministers have become increasingly critical of the performance of senior civil servants, especially over the implementation of large infrastructure projects.
- Ministers usually refuse to take responsibility for errors or delays by their department, instead, shifting the blame onto their senior civil servants.
- The permanence of civil servants is being eroded as ministers increasingly interfere in which officials are appointed to which posts. There is more movement in and out of civil service posts than ever before.

Also in 2013 the House of Commons Public Administration Committee produced a critical report on this relationship. Its key statement was this:

> We have found that both ministers and senior civil servants are still somewhat in denial about their respective accountabilities. The present atmosphere promotes the filtering of honest and complete assessment to ministers and is the antithesis of 'truth to power'. It is a denial of responsibility and accountability. There is a failure to learn from mistakes and instead a tendency to look for individuals to blame.

The main problem here is that, if civil servants are losing their anonymity and being made publicly accountable for decisions and policies, they will also lose neutrality. This is because they will want to direct ministers towards specific actions, rather than allowing ministers to decide. In other words, the new description of the relationship would be 'civil servants *persuade*, ministers decide'.

Box 9.1 Case studies

The Devereux case

The problem of relations between ministers and civil servants was highlighted when a public row blew up between work and pensions secretary, Iain Duncan Smith, and his most senior civil servant, the permanent secretary, Sir Robert Devereux, in 2013.

The government had been accused of seriously mismanaging the introduction of a new system of universal tax credits, a key element in the government's welfare reform programme. The Public Accounts Committee in particular accused the minister of presiding over delay and confusion in the new policy. Normally, according to the traditional principle, the minister should have made himself responsible. Instead Duncan Smith blamed Sir Robert and his colleagues for the errors and would not testify to the committee.

The implication of this was that it was the senior civil servants, and not the minister, who were making key decisions.

The West Coast railway line franchise

In late 2012 the government awarded the franchise to run the West Coast main railway line to FirstGroup instead of Virgin, who had run the line up to then. Virgin appealed against the decision on the basis that the Department of Transport had not examined the rival bid properly. It won the appeal and the whole process of awarding the new franchise was thrown into delay and confusion.

The Public Accounts Committee called the incident a 'fiasco' and the Transport Select Committee blamed the whole department for the errors. Labour accused the ministers concerned of 'hiding behind their civil servants', while ministers were blaming civil servants for the mistakes. The Public Accounts Committee was especially worried that the department was in no fit state to implement the High Speed 2 plan for new rail lines to Birmingham and the north.

The two case studies above demonstrate that there is now confusion over two issues:

1 Who should be accountable for serious errors — ministers or civil servants?

2 Who is responsible for key decision making? In the past we assumed that ministers make all final decisions, but this is thrown into doubt if ministers begin to blame civil servants for making bad decisions.

The cabinet minister who is responsible for the civil service, Francis Maude, has also entered the conflict by seeking reforms that will mean that ministers will have more control over the appointment of senior civil servants. Maude has also been critical of civil servants over the lack of support some have given to the coalition's financial policies.

Labour Party leaders have suggested that, if ministers do exercise greater control over senior civil service appointments, the service will no longer be neutral. In other words, if civil servants believe their jobs are at stake, they are likely to give information the minister wants to hear, rather than impartial advice.

The role of special advisers (also known as 'spads')

The growth in the use of special advisers in government over recent decades has largely been driven by ministers who have felt that they lack specifically *political* advice. There is certainly no shortage of *neutral* advice, which is provided by an army of civil servants, the permanent employees of the departments they lead. Political advice involves judgements that affect not only the national interest, but also the interests of the government and the governing party. As we have seen above, civil servants are not permitted to give such political advice so there was a large gap in the machinery of government. Special advisers have increasingly bridged this gap. To place this in an international context, the governing systems of France and the USA make extensive use of special political advisers. In France every minister has his/her own *cabinet*, an inner group of political advisers. In the UK there has been a reluctance to use special advisers, but this has faded so there are now nearly a hundred such individuals operating in Whitehall.

In 2012–13 the number of special advisers increased from 85 to 98. They only represent 2.2% of total senior servants, but their influence is considerable as they are in day-to-day contact with ministers.

Box 9.2 Spads — three case studies of their influence

Jeremy Hunt and Adam Smith

Adam Smith was Hunt's special adviser when Hunt was secretary of state for culture, media and sport. In 2012 Hunt, the responsible government minister, was asked to make a ruling (on a strictly neutral basis) on whether Rupert Murdoch's News Corporation should be allowed to take over BSkyB. The issue was whether such a takeover would create a monopoly operating against the public interest. It transpired that Smith, the relevant special adviser, had apparently been working behind the scenes to ensure the takeover was successful. This broke the neutrality rule in the minister's role. When the Leveson Inquiry investigated the matter, Hunt blamed Smith for the lack of neutrality and so escaped any personal responsibility for the poor conduct of the investigation into the proposed takeover. In the event, the takeover collapsed and Smith lost his job. Hunt kept his job, was not forced to resign and was later promoted to health secretary.

Michael Gove and Gordon Cummings

Cummings advised Gove on education matters. When he left the post in October 2013 he revealed that many of the policies of the department were failing. He said free schools suffered from poor teaching, that most of the Sure Start programme to help pupils from difficult backgrounds was largely a waste of money and that many higher education courses were irrelevant. More controversially, however, Cummings has argued that most educational ability among children is genetic, i.e. inherited. Such a belief flies in the face of most academic evidence and belief. It also suggests that most attempts to deal with low attainment are misplaced. What has alarmed observers is that a minister was being advised by a man whose views were at odds with government policy and were highly controversial in a scientific sense. This makes it extremely difficult to understand who should be called to account for education policy and its performance.

David Cameron and Christopher Lockwood

There is no specific controversy over Christopher Lockwood's appointment as a senior special adviser to the prime minister in April 2013. However, he is an old friend of the prime minister and his family, as well as of chancellor George Osborne. His appointment was widely seen as an example of 'cronyism'. A similar charge was levied against Tony Blair when he was prime minister. Lockwood also has a similar social background (public school and Oxford) to many other ministers and special advisers to the government, notably another of Cameron's advisers, Jo Johnson, the brother of London Mayor, Boris.

The issue that arises from the appointment of Christopher Lockwood and similar characters is the fear that there may be an 'inner circle' of special advisers, all socially linked to each other and therefore very close-knit and secretive. In other words, is this possibly hidden 'government within government', a group of policy makers whose role is not clear and who cannot be made accountable for the advice they are giving?

It should be stressed that this is not a new phenomenon. Blair consulted with an inner group of advisers, and the expression 'kitchen cabinet', meaning a group of personal advisers to the prime minister operating privately outside cabinet, dates back to Prime Minister Harold Wilson in the 1960s.

Summary

The fundamental problem that has arisen as a result of these developments and conflicts is that of **accountability**. Associated with this is the issue of **individual ministerial responsibility**.

The problem, in short, is this: if we do not know who is actually making decisions, be it ministers, civil servants or special advisers, we have great difficulty making anyone accountable for these decisions, especially when things go wrong. The select committees of parliament, to whom government is accountable, have experienced serious problems in locating the origins of many policies, decisions and management systems.

The principle of individual ministerial responsibility used to state that ministers are responsible for what goes on in their departments and must make themselves accountable for errors or mismanagement. Today, however, ministers are increasingly trying to make their civil servants accountable (or put crudely, 'blaming them'). The cases of the implementation of universal tax credits and the franchising of the West Coast main line, as described above, are prime examples of this problem.

Returning to the three principles of the civil service (see 'The traditional position of civil servants' section above), we can see that at least two of them have now been eroded:

- **Anonymity** is now destroyed by the fact that senior civil servants are often required to appear before select committees, whose proceedings are public, and by the fact that ministers are now more likely to name civil servants who, they feel, have made errors.
- **Permanence** is weakened because ministers are increasingly demanding that they should choose their own senior officials and that they should be able to dismiss or move civil servants who they believe to be under-performing or to be out of step with their own philosophy. If civil servants feel their position is insecure it may erode their neutrality.
- **Neutrality** is probably least affected. There is still a reasonably clear distinction between 'neutral' advice and 'political' advice, the former offered by civil servants, the latter by special advisers. However, as we have seen above, if ministers exercise patronage over senior civil servants, they are less likely to give neutral advice that the ministers might disagree with.

Exam focus

To consolidate your knowledge of this chapter, answer the following questions:

1 How has accountability been eroded in British government in recent years?
2 Is the doctrine of individual ministerial responsibility still relevant?
3 To what extent has the anonymity of civil servants now been abandoned?
4 In what ways do special advisers undermine the role of civil servants?
5 How has the relationship between ministers and civil servants changed in recent years?

Chapter 10

Rights: is the European Convention on Human Rights (ECHR) threatening state security?

Exam success

The up-to-date facts, examples and arguments in this chapter will help you to produce good-quality answers in your AS unit tests in the following areas of the specifications:

Edexcel	AQA	OCR
Unit 2	**Unit 2**	**Unit F852**
Judges and civil liberties	The British constitution	The judiciary

Context

The history of the European Convention on Human Rights (ECHR)

1950 The ECHR was first drafted by the Council of Europe (note: NOT by the EU).

1953 The ECHR came into force.

1959 The European Court of Human Rights was established to implement the ECHR.

1966 Britain signed the ECHR Treaty enabling UK citizens to take cases to the court for judgements. However, the ECHR was not binding in the UK, only advisory.

1998 The Human Rights Act was passed by the UK Parliament. This brought the ECHR into British law. It became binding on all public bodies including the government and the devolved administrations, but is not binding on the UK Parliament, which remains sovereign.

2000 The ECHR came into force in the UK. Since then, any British citizen has been able to bring a case under the ECHR to a British court (normally the High Court and/or the Supreme Court) and does not have to go to the European Court. This makes it quicker, easier and cheaper to bring such a case. The British courts also have to take the ECHR into account when reaching a decision.

What does the ECHR say?

The ECHR has 18 articles that establish a variety of rights. There are also 14 protocols. All member states of the Council of Europe have agreed to all the articles, but some have not signed up to all the protocols. Table 10.1 lists the articles most relevant to UK government.

Table 10.1 ECHR articles most relevant to UK government

Article 2	**Life.** Governments must not kill any citizen unlawfully, and should take steps to protect human life and to investigate unlawful deaths.
Article 3	**Torture.** Governments must not use any methods against suspected criminals or terrorists that could be defined as torture. This implies that courts cannot use evidence against a person that has been obtained by torture.
Article 5	**Liberty.** Citizens are entitled to be free and not to be imprisoned or held in any way without trial. They must be brought to trial within a 'reasonable time'.
Article 6	**Fair trial.** Various safeguards are in place to ensure trials are fair and everyone is treated equally, all shall have legal representation and trials should be held in public.
Article 7	**Retroactivity.** It is forbidden for a state to pass a law that applies to actions that were not, in the past, a crime at the time they were committed.
Article 8	**Privacy and family.** Widely interpreted to mean freedom from unwarranted searches of one's property, and protection from unlawful surveillance and from having information about a person held without their knowledge.
Article 9	**Conscience and religion.** The state must not prevent anyone following a religion or set of beliefs or prevent anyone from expressing religious views, provided these are lawful and will not lead to crimes being committed (incitement to crime).
Article 10	**Expression.** Provided any form of expression does not lead to a crime, does not slander or libel a person or might not lead to a danger to national security, there must be no state restrictions.
Article 11	**Association.** The state must not prevent any groups from forming associations, as long as such associations are not for the purpose of breaking the law or threatening the security of the state.
Article 14	**Discrimination.** No groups or individuals should suffer discrimination or unequal treatment by any public body.

What is the problem of the ECHR and national security?

Several of the articles shown above can cause problems for the UK state in its attempts to prevent terrorism and safeguard national security. Since 2000 when the Human Rights Act came into force and the ECHR was applicable in the UK, there have been a number of cases that have illustrated the issues. Some of these are described below.

Torture

Though there have not been many cases where the UK state has been accused of torture, this aspect has caused problems when the security forces are seeking to deport an individual who is wanted for trial abroad. Some of these individuals have been suspected terrorists. The most famous case was that of **Abu Qatada**, a Muslim cleric who was wanted for trial on various charges in Jordan. He was considered a danger to British security as he preached Islamic extremism. The British government was frustrated as the European Court of Human Rights ruled that he should not be deported as he might face evidence collected under torture. In the event the Jordanian government signed a treaty promising not to use such evidence and Qatada gave up his legal fight to stay and was deported. In general, deportation of individuals who are considered a threat to the UK is often difficult because of such restrictions.

Liberty

Here the issue concerns the meaning of the restriction that requires that a suspected person, including possible terrorists, be brought to trial within a reasonable time. The security services would like to hold suspected terrorists for long periods while they are questioned. Sometimes they cannot be formally tried because surveillance evidence cannot be used in court. The most celebrated case is known as the **Belmarsh Case**. In 2004 the House of Lords (which used to be the highest UK court of appeal before the Supreme Court replaced it in 2009) heard an appeal by nine men who were being held indefinitely at Belmarsh prison while they were being questioned on suspicion of terrorist activities. The court ruled that the men had to be released immediately or brought speedily to trial. As a result, suspected terrorists can now only be held for a maximum of 14 days without trial. The security forces argue that this is not long enough.

Privacy

Since a test case *S and Marper* v *UK* in the European Court of Human Rights (2008), it has not been possible for the police to retain the **DNA records** of people they have arrested or questioned, unless those people have been convicted of a crime. This makes it difficult for them to cross reference such records when they are dealing with suspected terrorists and criminals.

Family

In October 2013 the home secretary, Theresa May, lost an appeal in the Supreme Court when she was attempting to revoke the citizenship of a former immigrant. **Hilal Al-Jedda** was suspected of planning terrorist attacks against British troops in Iraq. He had been granted citizenship in the past and resided in Britain from 1992 to 2004 before the Home Office revoked his citizenship and sent him to Iraq. However, Al-Jedda had a family of eight children in Britain. The Supreme Court ruled he could return to Britain as the revoking of his citizenship made him stateless and prevented him from caring for his family. The government sees him as undesirable and regards him as a threat to national security.

Conscience and religion

Many argue that terrorism is being encouraged by so-called radical Muslim preachers. Because the ECHR guarantees freedom of religion it is difficult for the Home Office to silence them and close their mosques as this might infringe the terms of the ECHR.

What the politicians say

There has been a concerted attack by Conservative ministers on the ECHR, its European Court and the Human Rights Act. Two examples of this attack are given below, followed by a defence of the ECHR:

Chris Grayling, justice secretary, said in March 2013:

> I cannot conceive of a situation where we could put forward a serious reform without scrapping Labour's Human Rights Act and starting again. We cannot go on with a situation where people who are a threat to our national security, or who come to Britain and commit serious crimes, are able to cite their human rights when they are clearly wholly unconcerned for the human rights of others.
>
> Source: *Guardian*, 3 March 2013

Theresa May, the home secretary, added:

> We need to stop human rights legislation interfering with our ability to fight crime and control immigration. That's why, as our last manifesto promised, the next Conservative government will scrap the Human Rights Act, and it's why we should also consider very carefully our relationship with the European Court of Human Rights and the convention.
>
> Source: *Daily Mail*, 9 March 2013

Lord McNally, Liberal Democrat justice minister, said in defence of the ECHR:

> Of course our human rights legislation will defend criminal suspects but also the grandma in the care home, the child that has been abused; it will protect the right of people to protest against politicians. If we don't keep to the Convention, what hope is there for the gay man in Russia, for the political activist in Belarus? We have to be resolute in taking this on. We will be at the barricades and Liberty will be there with us.
>
> Source: speech at the Liberal Democrat Party Conference, 7 October 2013

Summary

Arguments against the ECHR

Clearly, the question of whether the ECHR is threatening national security has been answered with a firm 'yes' by most Conservatives. The summary of their criticisms includes these issues:

- It prevents the government deporting enough undesirable people. If such people have established a family here, or may face the death penalty abroad or a trial where torture has been used to gather evidence against them, the courts will invariably protect their right to remain in the UK.
- In some cases it may force the Borders Agency to accept immigrants or asylum seekers who are seen as dangerous, e.g. if they are joining family members already legally residing in the UK, or if they can show that their life is being threatened in their home country (note Article 2 of the ECHR, above).
- Under the terms of the Act it is difficult for the security services to bring suspected terrorists to justice. This is largely because they have to be released if not charged within 14 days.
- The tracking of suspected terrorists is made more difficult by the fact that DNA records can only be held on convicted individuals.
- The parts of the Convention that protect freedom of religion and expression mean that it is difficult to prevent religious leaders encouraging radical views that may lead to terrorism.
- There is an argument that if the security services are forced to present evidence in open court against terrorist suspects, this will compromise their identities and methods. The ECHR, however, insists that trials must be open.

Arguments for the ECHR

Those who defend the ECHR make two main arguments:

- Most importantly, they argue that rights cannot be sacrificed even for the sake of national security. If individual rights and freedoms can be threatened by government it represents the 'thin end of the wedge' towards tyrannical government. Such a tyrannical government, it can be said, would encourage rather than deter anti-state activities.
- Second, they argue that there is no reason why the security services should not be able to operate against terrorism within the existing legal constraints. For example, if the anti-terrorism authorities have gathered evidence against suspects, even through mobile phone records, they should be able to present such evidence in open court.

Exam focus

To consolidate your knowledge of this chapter, answer the following questions:

1 Why does the ECHR come under attack from Conservatives?
2 Explain how freedom of expression, association and movement are said to protect terrorists.
3 Make a case for retaining the ECHR.
4 What was the political significance of the Belmarsh Case?

Chapter 11

Briefings

This chapter will bring you up to date with some of the most recent political developments and demonstrate how they are relevant to your studies in government and politics.

Syria: has the historic Commons vote against intervention created a new constitutional convention?
(Topic: The UK constitution, prime minister and cabinet/core executive)

On 29 August 2013 the House of Commons held a vote on whether the UK should contribute to a US/French military intervention in the Syrian civil war. This was an unusual event as it is not normally the case that such a vote is required to sanction military action. The outcome of the vote was, to say the least, dramatic.

In the summer of 2013 the Syrian civil war had taken a turn for the worse when it was revealed that chemical weapons had been used against civilians, hundreds of whom had died as a result. There were widespread demands for intervention and, indeed, Presidents Obama of the USA and Hollande of France committed themselves to taking action against the Assad government which was accused of the atrocity. David Cameron declared that he was in favour of such action and then took a fateful decision. He decided to hold a vote in the House of Commons, seeking the approval of MPs. A combination of Labour, Liberal Democrat and small party MPs defeated the government's motion and so Cameron had to back down. After the vote he said:

> It is very clear tonight that, while the House has not passed a motion, it is clear to me that the British parliament, reflecting the views of the British people, does not want to see British military action. I get that and the government will act accordingly.

In the event, of course, no such intervention was needed. A Russian-backed compromise was agreed by the Syrian government to locate and then destroy stockpiles of chemical weapons. There was also an agreement by the Assad government in Syria not to use such weapons in the future. Neither the USA nor France intervened.

Why was this an important event in British constitutional history?
The answer concerns the common law principle of prerogative powers, which are exercised by the prime minister on behalf of the monarch. A key prerogative

power is that of acting as commander-in-chief of the armed forces. Normally such powers do not need the approval of parliament.

In the recent past, British prime ministers have certainly exercised this power without prior parliamentary approval (though advisory votes may have been held, the action did not depend upon them). Table 11.1 shows some examples.

Table 11.1 Acting as commander-in-chief of the armed forces — recent examples

1999	**Tony Blair in Kosovo** — for humanitarian reasons, to prevent the ethnic cleansing of Muslims by Serbia-backed forces.
2000	**Tony Blair in Sierra Leone.** British help was requested by the elected government of the country to help it fight off rebel forces and protect democratic rule.
2003	**Tony Blair in Iraq.** Blair joined the American invasion of Iraq to find 'weapons of mass destruction' (which were not found) and ultimately to remove Saddam Hussein from power. The action has since been widely criticised, though Tony Blair continues to defend it.
2011	**David Cameron in Libya.** Cameron agreed to use the Royal Air Force to help rebel forces that were beleaguered in the city of Benghazi. This was a successful action to ensure that Colonel Gaddafi was overthrown, on the grounds that he was a sponsor of terrorism.

Why was Syria different?

The answer probably lies with Blair's action over Iraq in 2003. His decision to join the invasion in the face of widespread opposition was heavily criticised. David Cameron possibly learned a lesson from Iraq and so sought parliamentary approval first. In other words, Iraq may have changed permanently the relationship between the prime minister and parliament.

It is too early to be sure, as constitutional conventions tend to develop over long periods of time, but we can now perhaps argue that a new convention is coming into being. This convention would be: *The prime minister requires the approval of parliament before undertaking any major military action, even though, in law, he is not bound to accept the outcome of such a vote.*

It will be some time before we can be sure that this is indeed a new constitutional convention.

Failing markets: what are the various ideological approaches to energy prices, the banking system and the housing crisis?
(Topic: Political parties)

In recent years Britain has seen major crises involving some of our largest private sector markets. Three examples are discussed here.

1 The energy companies

In a series of announcements in autumn 2013 the main energy suppliers (gas and electricity) announced a round of large price rises, in the approximate range 8–10%. There was an immediate outcry. There were accusations of profiteering and that the companies were insensitive to the plight of poorer families (poor families spend a high proportion of their income on energy and so are especially badly affected). This followed several years of large price increases.

2 Banks

Among many other concerns over the behaviour of banks there has been concern that the banks are not lending enough to small and medium-size companies and so are stifling economic growth. At the same time they are accused of not lending enough to house buyers, especially first-time buyers. A third issue has been the behaviour of so-called 'payday loans companies'. These companies charge huge rates of interest in return for lending to high-risk individuals. They have also been accused of making excessive profits and of callous behaviour.

3 The housing market

Despite the poor state of the British economy in recent years, house prices and private sector rents have continued to rise. The demand for housing exceeds the supply and it has proved difficult to promote increased house building. This means it is very hard for the young and low paid to find housing. By 2013 this was being described as a 'crisis'.

The common theme

These three problems have a common theme. This is that in all three cases, it appears the market is failing. What this means is that the normal economic processes that solve the problems are simply not operating. Normally, the market mechanism should ensure that when prices are rising, when there is a lack of competition and when demands of consumers are not being met, new companies should enter the market, bringing down prices and offering more choice for consumers.

The three main political parties have been forced to develop responses to these problems. In each case we can discern two categories of response. These are ideological responses and pragmatic responses. It is interesting to reflect on how the parties have responded in the light of this distinction.

Table 11.2 shows how the parties have reacted and demonstrates the distinctions between ideology and pragmatism.

Table 11.2 Political responses to market failures

Issue	Ideology 1: socialism	Ideology 2: neo-liberalism	Pragmatic response
Energy prices	The left-wing response would be to say that the market has failed and that this is typical of free market capitalism. Therefore, the energy companies should be nationalised (bought for the public by the state) and run in the interests of consumers and workers in the industry.	Neo-liberals (mostly Conservatives but also some Liberal Democrats) will say that the answer lies with *more* competition and less state interference, and that the market will sort itself out if left alone. Intervention by the state will not help. All the state should do is to remove any artificial barriers that exist which are preventing healthy competition.	This approach, largely that of the Labour Party but also partly supported by Conservatives and Liberal Democrats, rejects nationalisation. Instead proponents recommend that the market system should operate, but be regulated by the state to prevent profiteering and poor service. Initially this involves a cap on price increases, but in the long term means making it easier for consumers to switch suppliers and preventing excessive price increases.
Banks	Here again nationalisation is seen as most of the answer. Possibly state-run banks could be set up to compete with private banks.	Competition will eventually mean that banking will begin to serve borrowers more effectively. Thus small community-based credit unions should compete with payday loans companies. At the same time, new banks (such as Virgin and Metro) will compete with the big banks.	A healthy banking system has to be privately owned so no to nationalisation. However, competition is not working. Therefore the state must intervene to force banks to lend to small and medium businesses and house buyers at preferential rates. The government has adopted incentives to ensure this happens.
Housing	The main socialist solution is for the state to build houses and to rent them to families at subsidised rates (so-called 'social housing').	The free market is not working because there are too many regulations on house building and purchasing. So planning laws should be relaxed to allow more building, and stamp duty (tax) on house purchasing should be reduced or eliminated. This will boost house building, reduce the cost of purchasing and so bring down house prices.	While more building land should be released to increase the supply of houses, there should also be financial incentives for first-time buyers. Labour also wishes to release more funds for local authorities to produce social housing. This is a combination of state intervention and market forces working.

As things stand, the pragmatic approaches described above are dominant. They are supported by large groups within all three main parties. A small group within Labour wants to see the 'socialist' solutions used, but they are a small minority. The interesting question is how much the neo-liberal ideological approach will grow, mainly within the Conservative Party (the so-called 'Orange Book Group' in the Liberal Democrats also favour the neo-liberal approach).

Lewisham hospital: how has the latest judicial review against the government reignited conflict between judges and politicians?
(Topic: The judiciary and pressure groups)

In October 2013 the health secretary, Jeremy Hunt, lost an appeal against a judicial review that had gone against him earlier in the preceding summer. The issue concerned the part closure of the Accident and Emergency and Maternity wings of Lewisham Hospital.

The health secretary had argued that the savings obtained through the closure would lead to a generally better overall service. There was a sustained campaign by the hospital itself and a group called *Save Lewisham Hospital* against the proposed closures. These groups sought a judicial review, arguing that, under the terms of the National Health Services Act 2006, the secretary of state did not have the power to order such a closure. Thus the review was a so-called *ultra vires* case.

Jeremy Hunt appealed to the Appeal Court, but the judges upheld the original decision. This was hailed as a great triumph for the campaign groups and demonstrates how judicial review can be an important weapon in the armoury of many pressure groups, especially local ones.

The legal representative for the campaign group, Rosa Curling, said after the case:

> The decision to dismiss the appeal also reaffirms the need for judicial review, a legal process by which the unlawful decisions of public bodies, including the government, can be challenged by the public.

Reacting to the decision, Hunt commented:

> I completely understand why the residents of Lewisham did not want any change in their A&E services, but my job as health secretary is to protect patients across south London — and doctors said these proposals would save lives. We are now looking at the law to make sure that at a time of great challenge, the NHS is able to change and innovate when local doctors believe it is in the interests of patients.

Hunt's comment implied two things. First, he felt aggrieved that the advice of those doctors who advised him had been ignored. Second, he was hinting that the government might seek to change the law so that he *will* have power to order such closures. Despite the legal ruling, parliament remains sovereign and so can change the law to reverse the effects of this judicial review. Clearly, the case illustrates how an independent judiciary can interfere with the process of government if they feel that power is being abused. Yet critics may well say that key policy decisions like this should not be subject to such judgements from unelected judges.

Cabinet reshuffle: do the 2013 changes represent a breakthrough for Conservative women?
(Topic: Prime minister and cabinet/core executive)

David Cameron reshuffled his government in October 2013. The changes in personnel were not particularly controversial and certainly did not signal any major changes in government policy. However, one of the features of the reshuffle was the fact that it brought into government several new women. There had been criticisms that Cameron's government, particularly the cabinet, was too 'monotone', full of middle-aged white men from a private education background. The reshuffle improved the gender balance of government and also reduced its average age.

The new female members of government were as follows:
- Esther McVey appointed as minister of state (employment) at the Department for Work and Pensions.
- Nicky Morgan appointed as economic secretary at HM Treasury.
- Helen Grant appointed as parliamentary under-secretary of state (sport and equalities) at the Department for Culture, Media and Sport.
- Baroness Kramer appointed as minister of state at the Department for Transport.
- Baroness Stowell appointed as parliamentary under-secretary at the Department for Communities and Local Government.
- Jane Ellison appointed as parliamentary under-secretary at the Department of Health.
- Anna Soubry appointed as parliamentary under-secretary at the Ministry of Defence.
- Karen Bradley appointed as whip (Lord Commissioner).
- Amber Rudd and Claire Perry appointed as assistant whips.
- Baroness Jolly appointed as a whip in the House of Lords.

This appears to be an impressive number, but we should add two words of caution. First, the cabinet remains male-dominated. Only four of the 22 members are women. Second, the government as a whole is still dominated by men. The rise in the number of women was also made up of appointments mainly to junior posts. This has led to criticisms that the changes were largely cosmetic, a charge that was reinforced by the fact that two of the new women,

Anna Soubry and Esther McVey, are familiar faces, having been television presenters in the past.

The term 'breakthrough' would be something of an exaggeration. The Conservative leadership still retains its reputation of being resistant to women. This problem is exacerbated by the fact that so many members of the government were educated at private schools and so come from a privileged social background. But at least we can say that Cameron is aware that the social balance of his government needs to be adjusted (he also promoted a small number of MPs from ethnic minority backgrounds).

EU referendum bill: a rare example of a successful private member's bill
(Topic: The UK constitution, parliament)

On 29 November 2013, the House of Commons passed, without significant opposition, a private member's bill which would have the effect of forcing the government to hold a referendum on British membership of the EU in 2017. This would follow a renegotiation of the terms of membership. The bill was sponsored by James Wharton, a Conservative eurosceptic MP, but received the support of the government. Without government support, a private member's bill has little chance of passing, but David Cameron was content to allow James Wharton's bill through.

The Labour opposition and the Liberal Democrats were opposed to the bill but were also not prepared to vote against it, in case they were seen to be 'undemocratic'. Instead, they tried to delay the passage of the bill through various parliamentary devices so that it would eventually run out of its allocated time (the normal way in which a private member's bill is defeated). But all their efforts failed and the bill passed.

A number of problems and issues arise from the passage of this bill:
- It is rare for a private member's bill to succeed. So, whatever the final outcome, this demonstrates that it is possible for a backbench MP to promote legislation, but only if the government is prepared to stand back and let it happen.
- The bill also has to pass through the House of Lords. It is known that there is a good deal of opposition to the bill in the Lords and so its passage is far from assured. Mr Wharton, the bill's sponsor, said, 'For an unelected house to deny the British people a say on a bill which has been passed by the elected House of Commons, I think, would put them in a very difficult position.' This expresses the problem very well: will the House of Lords dare to deny the will of the elected House of Commons on such a key issue? Members of the Lords will counter the arguments by saying that the Commons has no democratic mandate to pass such a bill. It may result in a constitutional dispute between the two houses.

- If the bill does pass through the Lords and become law, it does not bind any future parliament to hold the referendum. The doctrine of parliamentary sovereignty means that 'parliament cannot bind its successors'. Furthermore, there will be a general election in 2015 so there will be a different parliament, and possibly a different government, by the time the proposed referendum is due in 2017. This means that parliament after 2015 will be able to repeal the EU Referendum Act so that the referendum will not take place. Having said that, it would be difficult for any future government to deny the people a say on such a key issue.
- If the bill becomes law and if it is not repealed by a future parliament, 29 November will prove to be an historic day. It might mark the beginning of a journey that could see the UK exiting from the European Union. James Wharton would go down in history, whatever else he may achieve in the future.

This bill will move to the House of Lords in early 2014. Whether or not it passes will largely depend upon the attitude of the crossbenchers who hold the balance of power there. The outcome may also be influenced by how well UKIP are doing in the run-up to the elections to the European Parliament in May 2014. UKIP, incidentally, oppose the bill on the basis that they believe there should be a referendum on British EU membership before the 2015 general election.

Scottish independence: Scottish National Party reveals its hand
(Topic: The UK constitution)

There will be a referendum on whether Scotland should become an independent, sovereign country on 24 September 2014. The Scottish National Party, the principal sponsors of the referendum who also lead the 'Yes' campaign, published their 'prospectus' for Scottish independence in November 2013. The document, titled 'Scotland's Future', sets out both the arrangements for a transition to an independent Scotland as well as the case for independence.

Much of the attention has so far been centred on the problems associated with transition arrangements. These reveal a good deal about the UK constitution and the ways in which it can be amended.

The main issues include these:
- Should there be a 'yes' vote, it is proposed that Scotland would become an independent country in March 2016. Many argue this does not leave enough time for the transition. The Scottish government argues that 18 months is the average time it took for several small countries to become independent (mostly from the Soviet Union), so Scotland could do the same.
- Scotland would remain a monarchy, with the UK Crown being the titular head of the state of Scotland (an arrangement quite like the one that currently exists in Australia). This raises questions about what role the UK monarchy would have, especially as it is proposed that Scotland will have a new codified constitution. The effect, it is believed, would be to make the UK Crown little

more than a figurehead. Certainly the current prerogative powers enjoyed by the UK prime minister could not be exercised in an independent Scotland.

- What currency will Scotland use? First Minister Alex Salmond is saying that Scotland will keep the pound sterling. If this happens, who is to control the currency? Will the UK Bank of England have any control over Scotland's finances?
- What happens to the national debt? Clearly some of the national debt is accounted for by Scotland. There will have to be hard negotiations about how much of the debt will be accepted by an independent Scotland.
- Will Scotland be able to join the EU? One argument suggests this would be automatic as long as Scotland accepted its obligations under the existing treaties. However, it is normal for new entrants to adopt the euro; Salmond is arguing Scotland would keep the pound. Furthermore, new applicants have to go through a long application procedure and their entry requires the agreement of all 27 members, unanimously. There is no guarantee that Scotland would meet these requirements, especially if it resists using the euro.
- There remain questions over whether Scotland will be bound by treaties signed in the past by the British government.
- The armed forces will have to be split to provide Scotland with some defence and security capability (though the Scottish government will not maintain nuclear weapons).
- There are problems over defining nationality. Who will be automatically Scottish? Will people have a choice? Will it be possible to have dual nationality?

There are many other issues which will need to be negotiated, including who will be responsible for paying state pensions, what will happen to oil being pumped from the North Sea and will Scotland be able to receive BBC broadcasts. So, even in the event that Scotland votes 'yes', there will still be many obstacles on the road to full sovereignty.

The chancellor's autumn statement: a new direction for policy?
(Topic: Political parties)

The chancellor of the exchequer's autumn statement was revealed on 4 December 2013. It sets out the future policies of the government in relation to taxation and public expenditure. This is a key political event as it will define much of the debate on economic and social policy in the run-up to the 2015 general election.

The key announcements were these:
- Those currently aged 40 or below will have to work to the age of 68 or 69 before they will become entitled to a state pension. This will effectively extend people's working lives by 2 years in the future.
- The deficit is not forecast to fall very much, so 'austerity measures' will have to continue for several years to come.
- Taxes on petrol will be frozen for the next year to keep fuel prices down.
- Employers will pay less National Insurance if employing young people.

- There will be a new married persons' tax allowance, creating a financial incentive for people to marry or stay married rather than merely live together.
- All infant school children will have free lunches.
- The threshold at which people start paying income tax will rise to £10,000 per annum. This will especially help the low paid and makes good a Liberal Democrat 2010 election promise.
- There are a number of technical changes designed to reduce tax avoidance.

Do these measures mark a change in policy direction? The answer has to be no. In fact, most of these measures have already been announced or indicated by government statements. The main features in terms of policy are these:

- It does recognise the importance of marriage, a key Cameron theme and consistent with traditional conservative values.
- There are some reductions in the tax burden for lower-income families and employers. This is very modest but is in line with the traditional conservative dislike of high taxation.
- It continues to emphasise the need to take strong measures to reduce the government deficit.

The main criticisms of the statement and of government economic policy in general include:

- It does very little (with the main exception of the freeze on petrol duty) to hold down the rise in the cost of living.
- It will do little to reduce growing inequality in the UK.
- It will condemn future generations to a much longer working life before they can claim a pension.

Thus the statement is consistent with government policies since 2010. The Conservative Party in particular will rely upon the fact that growth is returning to the UK economy and the financial deficit will eventually be reduced to persuade voters to support them in 2015. The question remains, however, whether people will support the party when they feel, for the most part, worse off than they did in 2010.